THREE ERAS OF NEW ENGLAND

AND

OTHER WRITINGS.

THREE ERAS OF NEW ENGLAND

AND

OTHER ADDRESSES,

WITH

PAPERS CRITICAL AND BIOGRAPHICAL.

BY

GEORGE LUNT.

BOSTON:
TICKNOR AND FIELDS.
MDCCCLVII.

PREFACE.

THE first three articles in this volume, together with that on a disputed passage of Shakespeare, never have been printed before. That which stands earliest in the order of arrangement was pronounced at the request of the New England Society of New York, in December, 1856. The author has thought it proper to retain, for this performance, the title under which it was written and spoken, although it will be seen, that a suitable reason induced him to modify somewhat his original plan. The second production was delivered a year ago, and also more recently on several occasions, as a Lyceum Lecture; and the third was given, also as a Lecture, before various similar associations, about ten years since. The Address, at the dedication of Horticultural Hall, originally published by the Massachusetts Horticultural Society, has been subjected to some slight changes, chiefly of expression, for the purposes of the present publication. The brief eulogy on General Taylor was offered to the Circuit Court of the United States for the First Circuit, at the opening of its session, July 15, 1850, while the author held the office of Attorney of the

1*

United States for the District of Massachusetts. The use already made of the other writings in the volume is sufficiently indicated in the introduction of each piece. Of the Lectures, it is proper to say, that portions, and, in some instances, very considerable portions, were omitted in the delivery.

CONTENTS.

THREE ERAS OF NEW ENGLAND, ... 9
USES AND ABUSES OF THE DAILY PRESS, ... 67
MR. MACAULAY ON WARREN HASTINGS, ... 111
DEDICATION OF HORTICULTURAL HALL, ... 177
PRESIDENT TAYLOR, ... 207
FISHER AMES, ... 215
CHARLES JACKSON, ... 233
LECTURE BY RUFUS CHOATE, ... 249
A SHAKESPEARIAN RESEARCH 258

THREE ERAS OF NEW ENGLAND:

A LECTURE,

DELIVERED BEFORE THE NEW ENGLAND SOCIETY OF NEW YORK, DECEMBER 3, 1856.

THE beginnings of a nation are necessarily small. I speak not more of its numbers, than of its condition and habits. Nature, at the commencement of all colonial existence, takes the place of art, and the wants of nature are few and simple. It is surprising how summarily a removal from that state of society, which may be styled the common round of civilized being, strips us of our acquired tastes, and of the customary usages of our lives, and even of many of our most ordinary necessities. Conformity with the mere absolute requirements of life becomes then the result of that law, which is emphatically the essence of reason. The object, for which we then erect the rude and shapeless hut, is, that we may be shielded from the unfriendly elements. And, then, the unhewn timber, or unchiselled stone serve the same purpose, in our behalf, as base and pediment, façade, colonnade, architrave and frieze, contrived by the inward-looking eye of genius and wrought out by the most curious manipulations of art. Our primary necessities, of—

food, clothes and fire,

we shall then reckon to be all honestly supplied, though the meat be not presented upon the burnished service, which illuminates the banquet, nor the garments glitter with the lustre of invaluable jewels, nor the genial warmth be tempered, equalized, and controlled by the application of any artificial aid.

Whenever this is the state of man, the impertinent fictions and weak sophisms of life die out. The borrowings and lendings of the human creature fall away from him, under the rigid discipline of primeval necessities, as the encrusting dirt, which bedimmed the diamond, is removed by the hard process, which reveals and confirms its inestimable price. The voice of the mountain winds would mock at the most indispensable and best-recognized trappings of polished society, as they rent them away, and fastened them fluttering in the crevice of the cliff, or, bore them onwards to the unknown wilderness, and would hail its very comforts with the shout and laughter of derision. And what more piteous spectacle could be exhibited, than the favorite of the most courtly circle, arrayed for triumphant conquest, sitting solitary and helpless in the desert, where life itself is only granted to the hands and eyes and nerves, which know how to reduce its rugged heart to a serviceable subjection?

So far, therefore, as our familiar and inherent characteristics, which form the very foundation of our nature, and make us good, or make us great, are liable to become diluted or perverted by the sophistications of social being, they may acquire an actual refreshment and renewal, under the severe and inevitable trials of colonial existence; and thus, from the corrupt bosom of an outworn empire may spring that newer, and more wholesome flood of life, which shall invigorate a world.

This, then, is the absolute law of all legitimate emigration, that it leaves behind it the weaknesses, the concretions and superfluities of artificial life, and founds its new existence upon an appeal to the primordial elements of natural society. Pretence, which so constantly dazzles the unthinking multitude, cannot stand a moment in the presence of a reality, of which daily experience compels the application of its entire physical, intellectual and moral development. Even wealth itself, that universal criterion of every civilized community, becomes only adventitious, where true worth and sterling sense are requirements of indispensable utility. Respect clings only to those qualities, which are valuable, because they are absolutely useful, and he alone, who surpasses his fellows in wisdom, knowledge, and the substantial attributes of heroic virtue, stands forth a king of men.

That most charming of all simple stories, of which boyhood never wearies, owes more than half its interest to the very principle I have suggested. This certainly does not result mainly from a consecutive relation of incidents, often trivial, and seldom claiming sympathy with what are commonly accounted our higher and more absorbing emotions. But it is, because we are taught to respect and value a human being, positively despoiled of every external aid, and reduced at once to the independent exertion of his intelligent faculties and capacities,—who thus conquers fear and weakness and the cruelty of fortune, and alone, amidst the utter solitudes of nature, becomes, in a far higher than any figurative sense, *the monarch of all he surveys.*

It is on this field, therefore, that the human character is not only tested, but developed and matured. For here, it is the inevitable tendency of life to revert to those fundamental principles, which we see only dimly through the mist and haze of artificial society. We are apt to believe, that the imagination of the poet alone must have invested the progenitors of a people with those attributes of greatness and heroism, which scarcely find any response amidst the hollow echoes of our own unreal hearts. We have been conversant with the weaknesses, the compromises, the pusillanimities, and the manifold perversions of social existence; we have looked upon its arrogant show, and have observed the success of those mere imitative propensities, which it accepts so readily as a substitute for sterling merit. We know how all these indications mark the outward progress, as they testify equally to the declining vital energies of a nation,—and we can scarcely conceive how there could have been behind us, in the far and twilight past, a passionate longing for the truth and an unshaken fortitude of soul,—a courage, a strength, a justice and a virtue, which were not then, if now, little more than irreducible abstractions, but as truly and necessarily the solid foundations of a rising state, as they are the adamantine pillars of universal and intelligent creation.

There may be more semblance of truth, therefore, than we sometimes imagine, in the crude memorials of remote antiquity; and the philosophic historian has wisely refrained from rejecting, as utterly fabulous, much which is commonly considered to denote only the age of fable. For uniform experience teaches, that some of our noblest qualities were exhibited under the severest pangs of penury and suffering, and often even those, which might seem half to warrant the traditional deification of demigods, whose uncertain characters loom up indistinctly through the shadows of distant centuries, or who still lower upon us, in imaged marble, from their crumbling pedestals.

And thus it may be, that the stern muse of early history intended only to characterize the idea of naked privation itself, in the exemplification of that savage nurse, around whose gaunt and shaggy bosom clung the infant arms of the founder of eternal Rome.

And this general view of the subject is susceptible of more or less faithful application to the early period of every people, which has laid the foundation of a flourishing empire amongst the unconventional simplicities of colonial existence,—not surely by reason of any conformity with the characteristic sordidness of savage life,—but, because sovereign nature, then sitting supreme, requires the manifestation of solid virtues, and of qualities, manly or womanly, as they should be; and demands and enforces a recurrence to those elementary and immortal principles, of universal obligation, which become refined away, or at least partially obscured, amidst the clashing relations, the gathering, varying and rapidly intermingling interests, and all the dust and struggle and fever of a progressive and sensuously practical and degenerately luxurious age.

That rugged integrity of the mistress of the ancient world, when, in the flush of her unblemished youth, she sought the sweet Egerian grot, to take counsel of more than mortal wisdom,—or that fundamental moral lesson, without which nothing is,—so impressed upon the still earlier Persian—*to speak the truth*,—in the palace, or on the plain, or as he ascended the mountain tops to hold communion with the stars,—are no more characteristic indications of the training of a mighty nation, than those weary years of the wilderness and painful wanderings of the chosen people, before their eyes were permitted to behold—

> Sweet fields beyond the swelling flood,—

which, by the irreversible covenant of ages, they and their children were yet to see

> Stand drest in living green.

But, certainly, never before so manifested, and quite as certainly, never again to be illustrated, in the same manner and degree, is that eminent exemplification of these principles to be found, in the settlement and progress of our beloved New England,—of that New England, to which our hearts turn with a devotion, which seems to us, at least, to be neither due, nor claimed, nor recognized by any other country or clime,—of that New England, to which her children, scattered, as many of them are, at the remotest extremities of the world, cling by peculiar ties and sacred associations and a closer kindred,—of her, whom we so love and venerate, as the common mother of us all—and so personify, under this familiar and endearing appellation, that, looking towards her from those places of exile, her hundreds of thousands of homes, scarcely divided from one another by any unfraternal wall of separation, seem all and each to be almost equally our own.

For never again can there be such preparation and such a result. No unexplored continent is again to cheer the eye of the long-baffled and almost despondent mariner—now doubted, as if it must be only some delusive cloud, and now re-hailed with the joyful cry of "Land!" as it rises, low and distant, under the eyelids of the morning, along the dim horizon of the dreary main. Never again, by some yet unborn Columbus, will a new world be given to the kingdom of Castile and Leon. Never again will human memorials be emblazoned with the enduring record of all their

> ———better fortitude
> Of patience and heroic martyrdom.

Never will be relighted the gospel-kindling fires of Smithfield,—never be rewritten a like-affecting story of the unexampled exile of Leyden,—never such a history of that one perilous traverse of the unknown deep,—instead of the southern verdure which hope had fondly anticipated and portrayed, to picture the bare, blank aspect of that wild, inhospitable sandcape,—to tell of the half-timorous yet half-hostile greeting of the savage, of the biting and bitter welcome of winter, and all from which the heart shrinks, as the eye wanders over that simple narrative, of dangers where there was no fear, and sufferings where there was no despair.

For my own part, I care little for the natural imperfections of such men. It is superfluous to defend the founders of New England. A vain and thankless task is his, who attempts to underestimate their virtues, or to detract from the majestic proportions of the gray fathers of the people. Their personal faults passed with them into the grave,—their just principles and noble actions survived and blossomed into a living harvest of sacred and immortal memory. Reversing emphatically the sad doctrine of the sentiment uttered over the dead body of Cæsar,—the good they did lives after them, while the evil, if evil there were, ended with their lives and is charitably interred with their bones. Their imperishable monument, not contracted to the too narrow dimensions of any mere material and precarious foundation, and exhibiting to the outward eye neither glittering shaft, nor airy pinnacle, is coextensive with the considerate judgment of mankind. More fortunate than the progenitors of any other race, there is neither obscurity nor uncertainty in the plain, clear and conscientious narration of their simple and pious annals; and no lapse of time can obliterate the undisputed memorials of all they were and did and suffered. If nothing else had ever been written in their favor, there are two records, at least, which will last forever to their praise. When the first colony, which fled from the persecutions of home, on the eve of their departure for their future habitation in the wilderness, was now about to bid that final and most affecting farewell to those hospitable arms which christian Holland had opened for their refuge, the magistrates of Leyden solemnly declared, that during their residence of twelve years, —which we well know were years of almost unparalleled trials and privations,—"these English" had not troubled the city with a single suit, or any sort of controversy; and the greatest historian of England, regarding their religious opinions with disdain and their political tendencies with a strongly-defined and systematic hostility, yet pronounces—"So absolute was the authority of the crown, that the precious spark of liberty had been kindled by the *Puritans alone;* and it was to this sect that the English owe the whole freedom of their constitution." To the peaceable, therefore,—peaceable, when no rights indispensable to peace itself were infringed,—and, thus minded, who assumed the sword, only that, by it, they might establish such tranquil rest as liberty alone allows, we owe that flame of freedom, which, but for them, had slumbered upon its embers throughout prostrate and oppressed Europe,—and another Christendom, to be purer, as they hoped, and more intelligent, as it well might be wider and mightier than the old.

From this point, therefore, we may fitly glance, for a single moment, over what may be justly entitled the

Primitive Era of New England. Assuredly, in no legitimate sense, can this be accounted a restoration of the Saturnian reign. As men ordinarily estimate happiness, the pilgrims of Plymouth, especially, were deficient in everything, which enters into the vague and illusory computation of external good. There was an almost total absence of what reality furnished, or imagination supplies, to complete the alluring picture of a golden age. Not only the softer delights of pastoral loveliness, but those grander developments, which at least dignify nature in some of the severest manifestations of her infinite moods, were equally wanting. No awful and cloud-crowned mountain, luminous with perpetual snows, glittered upon their enchanted vision,—no meadows spread before their eyes, enamelled with amaranthine flowers,—no rivers, clearer and purer than the bountiful bosom of maternal earth ordinarily vouchsafes, sparkled between emerald banks and over golden sands,—nor could they promise themselves to wander amidst consecrated groves, resonant with the intermingled harmonies of every airy melody and loaded with the lingering odors of a myriad fragrant beds of spontaneous bloom beneath. But they saw before them the low swell of the yellow sand-heap, and the dreariness of winter settling down in browner shadows upon the more distant hills—instead of the lustrous gleam, that rolls with the undercurrent of the azure river, blending its blue with gold, only the new-formed ice, that glittered upon the margin of every standing pool,—for meads embroidered with luxuriant flowers of every softest tint or deeper dye, nothing but the level of the desolate marsh, stretching far away, crested only with its unsightly patches of ragged sedge,—and for the lulling music of Arcadian woods, no song but the solemn requiem of long-departed Summer, breathed by the rising winds, in no gentle tones, to the responsive sighings of the November pines. Scarcely to the peal of triumphal hymns, therefore, but surely with patient and undaunted hearts, they found and thus chose their home, in the midst of a dreary wilderness, which promised absolutely nothing to their present necessities, but what the sad aspect of haggard want foretold, under the dispensation and infliction of real suffering. And yet, in the presence of such a scene, upon the deck of their frail vessel, at her moorings, before the first footstep had consecrated that 'Forefathers' Rock,' to be forever afterwards the very altar-stone amongst the memorials of that lonely harbor,—looking truth steadfastly in the face, and with a wiser forethought of the true condition of man than theirs, who imagine a primeval society of natural, unrestrained and therefore impracticable human freedom,—they drafted and executed, as never was such instrument made before, —that brief and noble declaration of principles, looking to the future formation of a frame of civil government, which should be known to all succeeding times as the Constitution of the Mayflower.

But though they thus settled upon the doctrine of a polity worthy of the sagest men of state, the star in the West, which they had seen, signified to them only security from religious persecution. No mere worldling is competent to the just estimation of characters quite out of the scope of his vision, whether he be known under the title of philosopher or historian. They cannot be judged, according to the ordinary rules of worldly prudence, for the only prosperity they sought was the rest of their souls. As literally as Jacob in the house of Egypt and the presence of Pharaoh, they counted the days of their years but the progression of a pilgrimage,—few and evil in the computation of their sum, and each in succession but bringing them, on the foot-road of a toilsome journey,

—a day's march nearer home.

Actuated and governed, in a great degree by the same general motives and principles, yet one chief object of their compatriots of Massachusetts was undoubtedly to build a state. And, as that chosen barque, which first settled down with her precious-freighted souls upon their Ararat of Plymouth, bore the charming name of the freshest flower, which peeps out of the chilly bosom of our New England spring, so the flag-ship of that little squadron, which first cast anchor beneath the shadow of those three lonely hills, looking down to-day upon the commerce of a world, must be forever associated with one of the sweetest of her sex, a lovelier flower,—in the narrow judgment of earth only too early transplanted to the skies. I read the admirable letter of those adventurous and high-toned men, to "the rest of their brethren in and of the church of England," from the cabin of the Arbella,* lying in Yarmouth roads,—and regarding that christian resolution coupled with humility and charity, and the self-sacrificing spirit of those "persons of worth and quality," as they were then styled, who came with Winthrop and Saltonstall and Johnson and Dudley and Vassall, and the rest,—who, on the eve of an enterprise, which, to have engaged the attention of such men, must have seemed to them great, were looking forward to a dwelling-

* I so write the name of this vessel, rather than "Arabella," in deference to the critical judgment of Hon. James Savage, the learned editor of Winthrop's History of New England, and to the cotemporary evidence of its correctness, which he adduces in the first volume of that invaluable work. But there is still another reason for this, which some may think even more conclusive. Arbella, it seems, was the designation of a certain district or locality of Judea, eastward beyond Jordan, and considering the marked preference of the Puritans for Scripture names, or such as had a bearing on Scripture, they would have been very likely to select this, for that reason; especially, since the word, Arabella, might involve an idea, in some sense offensive to their peculiar notions. Besides, Arbella is, I presume, the original word, of which the other may have been formed, for the sake of euphony, or by corrupt usage, at some period, either earlier, or more probably later than their day.

place in what they call their "poore cottages in the wildernesse,"—and who, however exalted in mind and reproached for spiritual pride, declare that they "are not of those that dreame of perfection in this world,"—and, methinks, in their case, there was, in combination with their religious hopes, the impulse of generous motives besides and a manifestation of great and noble characteristics, broader if not higher, than all which has been justly claimed for those pilgrims of Plymouth, whose first track, like a new star-beam over the waste of ocean, bridged it forever with inextinguishable light. And this Massachusetts, which thus they made their own, is truly the mother of New England; for hers were all its colonies, either by the natural and direct relations of offspring and home, or else, in one particular instance, by the bestowal of her maternal adoption and by filial submission to her control.

There are a great many false notions and partial views prevalent, in regard to the character and condition of these fathers of a new world. One would imagine, that any philosophical analysis of the motives and qualities, which must have laid at the foundation of such an enterprise, would have freed them from many misapprehensions and imputations, to which they are even now too often unjustly exposed. In regard to the social position of the main body of them, at home, in a mere worldly point of view, I am no more anxious than they were. But for their personal merits and accomplishments, for the elements of their private characters,—for those intellectual and moral traits, by which they were wiser and better than the founders of any other commonwealth, we may justly cherish the same elevated regard, which animates every grateful heart, in remembrance of its participation in any high and great and permanent good. Upon any fair and just view of their purposes, I am not willing to consider those men fanatics, who submitted to every personal privation for the sake of freedom of conscience, and for this great end, voluntarily separated themselves, by an ocean rolling between, from all those, to whom their conduct could give offence. Nor will I call such persons bigots who, having encountered and endured all things, to secure a liberty, precious, peculiar, and as they deemed it without controversy essential to their own spiritual welfare,—would not permit it to be disturbed, perverted, or wrested away, by self-willed intruders of whatever sect or degree, to whom the world of the wilderness was as open elsewhere, as it had been to themselves. The liberty of conscience which they sought, judging of it only for such spiritual needs as souls like theirs would crave, was liberty for their own conscience and not another man's. If they and their associates, who still remained behind, had been made of that stuff, which some men call liberal, because, being lukewarm in itself, it is equally unconcerned about every mode of faith,—then, truly, the church would have been troubled with no worse heresy than vice, the authority of court and star-chamber had been kept as undisputed, as it was insufferable and despotic,—Archbishop Laud had never stretched forth his hand to stay the interrupted embarcation of that one company of nonconformists, above all others, to the thunder of whose squadrons all Europe so soon listened, as, beneath the hoofs of their horses, hierarchy and crown were trampled into the dust,—no disciplinary axe had turned its sharpened edge against that "gray discrowned head,"—there would have been no approximation made to a settlement of the wise and just principles of religious liberty, and no impulse afforded to the spirit of civil freedom throughout the world.

The English moral poet somewhat impertinently declares—

Most women have no characters at all!

If he had pronounced a similar judgment upon a majority of the other sex, it would have been almost equally just. But those, of whom I have been speaking, had character,—individual, strongly-marked, peculiar,—resulting from reflection moulded in suffering, and heightened, if it could not be perfected, by religious experience. I consider these men great, therefore, who were directly or indirectly concerned

3

in the most momentous revolution of opinions, which has affected, or is likely to affect modern history; great in their simplicity, in their integrity, in their sacrifices and their struggles, and, above all, in that unimpeachable sincerity of character, which is the true secret of their greatness, as it is the earnest of every other virtue. Whatever might have been their particular grade in the social circle, the men, who were the instruments in such undertakings, were not of the ordinary stamp. Education they certainly had, in all that the schools of Europe then could teach, more or less generally diffused amongst them, and no true son of New England can fail to honor them, for the value which they so early and constantly manifested for its advantages and its transmission. Plain as they may seem to a superficial view, there was anything in their company but a deficiency of the graces of refinement and cultivation, and assuredly many of their leaders were distinguished by the profoundest learning of the times and the noblest intellectual endowments. Some of them, certainly, were persons of liberal fortune and of public and private eminence,—others had left all their fortunes and every worldly expectation behind them. There were few or none of them either of that highest class, too much absorbed in mere frivolities, or inextricably involved in affairs of state, or bound to the soil by hereditary ties and duties, incapable of release,—and they were far above that lowest order, which is generally beneath the operation of exalted impulses and noble motives. But the friends of Bradford and Brewster and Standish and Vane and Winthrop and others, who came, and of Brook, of Say and Sele, of Pelham, and Hampden and Pym and Haslerig and Cromwell, who were kept at home for the completion of other great cotemporaneous undertakings, measured by the standard of any just comparison, were anything but mean men.

We shall find few historic names in their records. They were of Saxon, not of Norman origin. But they were in general of that sturdy, middle class, between the high and the low, — husbandmen or rural proprietors, without whose manly characteristics and substantial nerve and muscle, there could have been no historic names, nor any of that history which dignifies a nation. They had as good soldiers in their company as divines, and laymen of various pursuits and occupations. They cannot be called men of peace, for that motto of Massachusetts, which Sydney originally inscribed at one of the passes of the Alps, shows that they understood the uses and necessities of war; and, indeed, their whole colonial existence was little else than one long warfare, for a period of more than a hundred and fifty years. Men of their stamp and degree, such as subsequently furnished the soldiers that Cromwell trained to victory, the countrymen and ancestors of the first settlers of New England, must have been found always, wherever the arms of England had acquired their old renown; of that order which so often, in the language of a cotemporary historian, "had made all France afraid,"—few in numbers, but invincible in courage —on the famous fields of hard-won battle, where their warrior-kings would have no more men to divide the honors of the day—

> *When* Valois braved young Edward's gentle hand,
> And Albert rushed on Henry's way-worn band,
> With Europe's chosen sons, in arms renowned,
> Yet not on Vere's bold archers long they looked,
> Nor Audley's squires, nor Mowbray's yeomen brooked,
> They saw their standard fall and left their monarch bound.

I endeavor to imagine the condition of the colony, a few years after the first sharp pinch of their almost desperate necessities was past. They were still, as they long continued to be, only a garrison in the wilderness. Up to the period of 1640, it may be safely computed, that the entire population of New England, capable of bearing arms, did not vary much from the tale of five thousand souls. And history, surely, offers no parallel to the fact of such an adventurous foothold, so marvellously gained and kept in the very face of a numerous savage people, whose tendencies, at least, were hostile, whose friendship was uncertain, whose treaties could only be reckoned each a hollow truce, whose very nature called for the domination of fear, who could scarcely have discerned the not very obvious advantages to themselves of yielding to the influence of conciliatory appeals, and who possessed the physical power to overwhelm their scattered handful of neighbors, to the human eye so apparently feeble, at any chosen moment. But the estimate, put upon them, by the early settlers of New England, seems to have been made up of a mingled sentiment of compassion for their heathenish ignorance, contempt for their divided and broken strength, and a guarded dread of their treacherous and lurking instincts. But indeed these men were valiant, strong and of good courage. And taking into consideration their true condition, their insignificant numbers, their inadequate means of defence, and that long siege of unexampled perils, through many weary, painful, watchful years, I count them brave with a more than mortal valor. They were frugal,—for, descended of a nation very far from opulent, and in which the means and sources of its subsequent wealth had only just begun to be developed,—and of a class, amongst which necessity had long taught and systematized the practice of a severe frugality,—upon them this rugged virtue imposed a still harder hand,—for, besides that sweat of the brow, which the primal curse, now almost converted into a blessing, entails, the very cultivation of their fields was often like the crimson harvest of arms. The seed of peace, which they had planted in trembling hope, was gathered in like a forage; and frequently they ate the scanty bread, thus wrung from an ungenial soil, sown, as it were, with armed men, at the imminent hazard of their lives. Wise they were, for clearly recognizing the spiritual elevation of mankind, as the only legitimate object of human discipline, they first sought the means for the advancement of whatever is to remain to the intellectual and moral being, when human discipline is at an end,—and looking far into the future, they endeavored thus to establish, upon broad and immoveable foundations, the substantial happiness of a long-coming posterity. I venture not to enlarge upon their piety,—if they were not pious, no men and women ever were!

I see that simple structure for religious meeting,—spireless, and, I doubt not, comfortless enough to the outward man,—to which as external, and therefore not vital,—in entire consistency with their views of those corruptions of the establishment, which had made the term, so applied, odious in their ears, they refused the name of "church." I presume, in correspondence with a not uncommon fashion of their rural descendants, it was frequently "set upon a hill,"—not merely that they might fulfil, in a strictly literal sense, the beautiful figure of Scripture, but in order that the sentinel at the door might command ample survey of the surrounding country, while his armed neighbors were devoutly worshipping within. I see a military captain of very tender conscience, resolutely cutting the cross from the "meteor flag of England," because he could not endure to march under such a relic of antichrist,—and the magistrates, tenderly considering his motive, while they rebuked the offence itself, since their consciences happily were a little more enlightened. I remark, in illustration of their primitive ways and condition, that the first Governor of Plymouth Colony was taken with his fatal illness, while he was laboring with the rest of the settlers in the field; and that, during the first hard winter, their hearts sank at the discouraging tidings, that this head of the state had the last batch of bread in the oven,—and that the first Governor of Massachusetts, seeing that the people of Ipswich were destitute of a minister, travelled to that village from Boston on foot, spent the Sabbath with them, and "exercised by way of prophecy." I read with pleasure, that, some years afterwards, when the latter dignitary, as deputy-governor, was exposed to certain injurious charges, he descended from his chair of magistracy, which was a literal, not a figurative upper seat, against all remonstrance,—and though "many of the court and assembly," we are told, "were grieved about his being in that place," put himself at the bar of the accused,—and upon his triumphant acquittal, delivered a speech seldom, if ever, surpassed, for its manly eloquence, its dignified humility,—its just, liberal, simple and yet statesmanlike views of the great and still misunderstood relations of human society. I contrast the too common impression, of the harsh lineaments of these severe Puritans, with their profound and affectionate lamentation over the death of a noble lady of their company, who, in their own language, had come "from a paradise of plenty into a wilderness of wants." And I see these men, too often reputed only cold, sectarian, narrow bigots,—sour in external demeanor, and inwardly almost divested of every human affection,—upon the arrival of the wife of their chief magistrate, in the midst of many distresses, gallantly assembling to "entertain her with a guard and divers vollies,"—and magistrates and people bringing together such great store of bodily comforts, to attest their welcome, "so as the like joy and manifestation of love had never been seen in New England."

It has been the general policy of warfare and of diplomatic negotiations, to set those forces at variance with each other, whereof the combined relations might be deemed of probable disadvantage to the negotiating party. But, so far as I know, it was reserved for these just men, fearing God and knowing no other fear, to manifest the highest principles of equity, by mediating for the pacification of savage tribes, hostile to themselves and hostile to each other, and whose passions, by the superior artifices of civilization, might have been easily wrought upon, for the benefit of the colonists and their own extermination. When no efforts at conciliation were found to be of any avail, I observe their resolute execution of their necessary purposes towards an inveterate foe. And, in illustration of this element of their character, I should be glad to linger a moment, if it were possible, over that most romantic and touching episode of their history, which an illustrious countryman of our own—too illustrious in the literature of the world, to permit you to claim for him anything more than the honor of his birth, has made forever immortal, in his beautiful memorial of Philip of Mount Hope.

I run through the stormy current of our colonial history,—the narrative of their conflicts and apprehensions of conflicts with domestic and foreign enemies—the Indian, so often made to yield and the Spaniard, whom they, at one time, dreaded,—of very headstrong and wilful-minded Dutchmen, whom they subdued by themselves, and querulous, reluctant Frenchmen, whom they reduced to subjection in their strongholds, or aided their countrymen from home to vanquish, upon their most inaccessible and formidable heights. I read of their truly independent political condition, prudently and sometimes with difficulty upheld, against the influence and evil speech of zealous foes at home, as they lovingly called the motherland,—and the jealous care, though more frequently the generous countenance, if not encouragement and support, of its own distracted state and varying government; and of that long interval, when the desperate struggles of England happily left them to the maturer development of their own resources. I imagine their steadily advancing strength and stability. I see the huts, in which they first sought refuge, gradually yet rapidly exchanged for those quaint gable-roofed and oddly-projecting dwellings, of which relics yet exist, going back to a very early period, in some of our older towns,—exhibiting no very accurate coincidence with the models of classic architecture, but which really seem to me far more picturesque, than the blank aspect of many modern edifices. They break through the forest, by a thousand difficult and dangerous paths,—the garrison-house becomes only the occasional place of refuge, instead of the necessity of nightly resort,—the close stockade gives place to the open street of the long, straggling village, or to the remoter settlement, or the lonely and still perilous farm-house,—and the buff-coat, thick enough and tough enough to turn away any ball, which any powder of that day could have had force enough to propel, and which, as I have actually set eyes upon it, must have completely enveloped the person of the redoubted warrior, whom it protected in his Indian conflicts, eventually yields to less voluminous habiliments.

I see them wise, therefore, and brave and frugal and just and pious, with the characteristic attributes of heroes and statesmen and, if you please, of Christian martyrs themselves,—and, for the sake of these fundamental virtues of humanity and distinguishing elements of greatness, I am willing to overlook very much, which, in their day and our own, has been too readily charged against them,—the banishment of a quaker or two, now and then, who innocently persisted in abiding under a jurisdiction, which, in accordance with what their judgment deemed essential to their own civil and religious peace, could not countenance and deliberately repulsed him; and who only persisted in returning, over and over again, to bear his somewhat officious and foolhardy testimony against those, who had solemnly forbidden him to come, on pain of death,—or other errors of the times, in falling into delusions, which I confess seem to me quite excusable, under the circumstances, in comparison with some, which people of reputed intelligence subject themselves to, in our own enlightened day,—or, the close-cut hair, the short cloak, (so lately revived) the Geneva band, the formal ruff and beard, and the heavy-hilted, perhaps rusty, but undoubtedly serviceable rapier of the one sex; and, of the other, the prim cap, the dress, more completely if not more gracefully than now adapted to the form, the unadorned loveliness, and the show of only just so much lace and trinketry, as the dames or damsels of the day could persuade, I fear only too successfully, some of the more tender-hearted amongst the worthy magistrates, to permit them to display.

And, upon any just judgment of the ordinary progress of human affairs, for what speculative failure they can be properly accounted responsible, I do not know, —these founders of a Puritan Commonwealth, whose system was necessarily modified by advancing time and opinions,—who thus took possession of so considerable a region of an uncivilized hemisphere, and so maintained themselves, under all sufferings and against all conflicts and discouragements,—who established principles of civil government still subsisting in their original force, and chiefly by their means diffused over a nation of free institutions,—who developed a religious character, yet venerated by a vast majority of their descendants, and, in spite of declensions, to which their own, like every other community, must have been subject, still seriously affecting the minds and conduct of their posterity,—and who entered into a civil compact, of mutual defence and offence, of such binding virtue and obligation amongst themselves, that the distinctive features of the alliance, though not formally acknowledged now, and though practically superseded by State and National Constitutions, yet, in no merely theoretical sense, remains, —making that population, so feeble only a little more than two centuries ago and now reckoned by millions, still a peculiar people within the bounds of its own territory, remarkably concordant in opinion on topics of public interest or importance, whether right or wrong; and making the children, who go out from it, to whatever other state or distant country, to retain, in a singular degree, and after the lapse of many years, the habits and thoughts, the feelings and affections of New England. So that, under this venerated name, she holds her reputation, which, more than upon any present intelligence, enterprise, prosperity or power, rests upon the character of the ancestors of her people, resulting from their solid virtues and substantial wisdom; but a reputation, which must be necessarily forfeited, as these ennobling elements decline.

It has been so much a labor of love with me, to contemplate at some length this primitive era, that I find it necessary, at this point, to change the title of my Lecture, and passing completely over one period, —though less necessary, as being more familiar,— which I had intended to consider, for a while, under the character of the heroic, to proceed at once to the third, which I shall denominate *the practical*, though many are fond of calling it *the intellectual* era of New England.

We launch, then, upon a wider and deeper sea,— and, pondering boldly, let us ask what there is valuable of the past, since such was the past, which this broad, grasping and insatiable present profitably retains. For I suppose, that even the most enthusiastic disciple of progress, who thinks at all, does not imagine that man,—the human being, who has fulfilled his generations upon earth, now for six thousand years, imprisoned for life in this single planet, and possessed only of certain definite capacities, is absolutely to drop, like a serpent his slough, all the experience of his race, together with their hereditary and constitutional characteristics, and to walk forth, regenerated and disenthralled, towards some unknown and indeterminate point, upon the desolate ocean of adventurous discovery.

What we have been considering hitherto was undoubtedly definite,—the qualities sound and positive, the virtues substantial and actual. The persons contemplated were men and women, committing errors unquestionably, but still their characters were true, and they themselves meaning something real, and working consistently to that end. If they were overformal in their manners, this slight discrepancy with a more modern recklessness of demeanor resulted from a deep sense of personal responsibility, controlling and attempering outward demonstration,—and, if precise in opinions, and their consequent mode of expressing them, it was because, turning neither to the right hand nor to the left, they earnestly sought to see clearly and so to speak of the nature and obligation of the highest conceivable duties. And if they were in truth good and great, it was because, endeavoring to leave behind them, so far as it was possible, in a world, the public and private duties of which they never neglected or disdained, the beggarly elements of mere worldly ways, they did actually and personally strive for a superior virtue and a superior intelligence. And since a combination of these two must form the supreme rational object of human existence, and, thus sought, explains their remarkable traits and the accomplishment of those aims, which were the wonder of their own day, as they will be the growing admiration of all future time, it would seem, that any observable deterioration, on our part, must imply a failure to follow in the same steadfast pursuit of substantial *good.* For this grand and universal object of every intelligent human soul, which a thousand philosophers, groping blindly throughout the universe, and countless generations of men have equally failed to discover, they sought only, where only it could be found, in the inmost depths of their own spiritual being.

So far, then, as analogy avails, I should hesitate to look into a state of society, which calls itself practical, for the most extraordinary developments of character and the highest manifestations of intellectual power. And yet we know that all sinks, or has sunk, where these are absent. The level surface is in reality stagnant. There must be something high in thought and action, or all things will be equally low. Men are either aiming for great things, or they are content with small. Society either advances, or it recedes. It will not do for it to settle down upon mere absolute realities, so called—repressing all the human host of spontaneous and perhaps unintelligible desires, which are still so suggestive of nobler and purer, if as yet unsatisfied sympathies. For, to do so, let me remark, is materialism—and materialism, tricked out in whatever external decorations or mere intellectual refinements, is but a turn of the corner to barbarity itself. And however decent even such a world may outwardly appear, within it is full of dead men's bones and all uncleanness. It would be like the loathsome creatures of the earth crawling amidst violets,—delicacy, and fragrance and loveliness and bluest bloom above,—beneath, poison, distortion, and disgust.

I am perfectly willing to yield to the spirit of the times every vain or seemingly unprofitable illusion,—if I can only be informed by some clearer-minded realist, than it has yet been my fortune to meet, what are the illusions and what the realities of this mortal state. I know that those of its things which are ordinarily accounted civilization,—its palaces and temples and freighted ships and warehouses opulent with the riches of nations, and its clasps of communicable iron, interlacing and girdling an empire, and even its intellectual speculations into the abyss of the unknown,—may be only deceptive indications, and not its undoubted proofs. I know that civilization does consist of liberty and order, and harmonious thought and feeling, and refinement and virtue,—and that the perfection of these excellencies demands the cultivation of all the immortal capacities of the mind and heart,—and that, for want of our means, in this behalf, no nation of the heathen world ever did or ever could reach, or even imagine, that standard of general elevation, set forth for the example and attainment of a Christian age. I know, moreover,—because reason and observation and experience coöperate to teach the salutary lesson,—that these characteristics of a people are no more developed and sustained by the keenest faculties, ever sharpened in the collisions of the market or the contests of the forum, than by the numberless and nameless graces, which owe their birth to our imaginative perceptions,—by the infinite and vague emotions of the spirit within us, impressing upon the forms of things, as well as it is able, the pictured image of its own unsatisfied longings,—or by the solitary contemplations of the student of nature and of art, moulding the means and ends of life into the shapely proportions of a model, quite beyond the reach, it may be, of that practical conception,—around whose knotted hardness they yet verdantly and benevolently entwine all life itself can know of grace and blessing and joy.

But the age of reality should, at least, be the age of certainty. And, as a lover of truth and a lover of my country, I should be glad to learn, if possible, in the investigation of this subject, what reasonable prospect there is in the future, for certain improvement in law, and order and government, and mind and morals,—in social opinion and social virtue, and whatever else may be the fundamental elements of happiness and prosperity,—under a condition of things, which I think the general judgment would pronounce more unsettled than ever before. We do not need to go to the lessons of philosophy in order to ascertain, that intellectual pride and conceit and self-sufficiency are neither the sources, the means, nor the evidences of knowledge; and that presumption is a mark of weakness, tending to deterioration, and not of strength, giving promise of future good. It is an unfavorable state of society, which prides itself on being better than the past,—for then it is likely to be contented with inferiority, and, having no motive for improvement, it actually recedes. That individual man cannot and will not learn, who believes himself already quite above the mark of whatever has been attained by others in ages before. To him, the pursuits of those, who yet anchor themselves upon established truth, may seem little better than superfluous. And yet he may find that the probability of his own superior progress is an important question, not yet, perhaps, so conclusively settled.

It does not follow, that society is in a more healthy condition, because a certain amount of general practical information, of greater or less tenuity, is diffused over the surface of the community. There still may be dreary barrens and dismal depths, in the one aspect, and, in the other, no mountain of refuge, or any projecting cliff, to which we can fly for safety in the storm. The return to practical materialism is much more easy than many imagine. And, if we, looking only towards the future, reject that wisdom of the Past, which in morals and the science of the mind, at least, is the true basis of knowledge, it is not too much to say, that our descendants, growing gradually shallower and more shallow, may find themselves, at length, slumbering in the twilight of an age, than which no other has been more dark. And all our exterior splendors would no more indicate refinement, or secure freedom, than the magnificent ecclesiastical edifices of former times,—than the palaces of oppressed Italy, than the cathedrals of degraded and distracted Spain.

But, in fact, we do not, each and all, know by transmission, whatever has been learned and known before. This is not a present convertible possession of the world, upon which we can count, as an inheritance, to be the readily-employed stepping-stone to future acquisitions. The ordinary physical improvements in the usages of life can be reduced, indeed, to common practice and diffused,—so that much, which tends to our external comfort, and was altogether beyond the possible imagination of ruder times, becomes the general property and contributes to the universal welfare,—although nothing could be easier, than to show an almost total ignorance of, and indifference to, the most manifest improvements, even of this description, within the circle of our own ordinary observation. But the triumphs of intellect and the attainments of virtue are reached only by a very different process. For these are severally to be gained by every individual man, in his own generation, or not at all. In these there is no common stock. His training in these respects must be as much his own, as if nothing had been accomplished, in all past time;—and, for all that has gone by, there are tens of thousands in the streets and hovels of this city, to-night, who are neither wiser nor better, than the least-considered of their predecessors, a thousand years ago. I am no better, individually, for the moral precepts of every age of the world,—no wiser for its learning, its science and its literature, unless their truths and excellencies and results have each been sought out and applied by me, individually, for myself. And, although science, certainly, as being concerned more directly with the outward necessities of our nature, has crowned its eminent explorers with their fame and their reward, yet too much neglect of the obviously intelligible doctrine I have suggested may account for other deficiencies, which have been thought to denote the declining, rather than the essentially progressive character of the age.

The popular theory, in one class of modern society, unquestionably is, that man, under the action of certain mysterious influences, as yet only imperfectly developed, and how to be developed even, does not yet appear, is eventually to become something in the scale of intelligent being, which he never yet has been. I do not know to what definite extent this idea has been carried, or what accurate notion has been formed of this physical phase of progress. So far as I do know, the algebraic formula as yet exhibits only an unknown quantity. But it has been quite sufficient, certainly, to disturb and unsettle, to no inconsiderable extent, the surface of the mind of New England,—so that vague speculation, upon important subjects, if nothing worse, has either eradicated, or essentially modified, ancient well-defined convictions, by which its population was formerly marked, and which undoubtedly made one chief element of its real or presumed superiority.

For my own part, entertaining great diffidence in regard to the perfectibility of human nature, if anything seems apparent to my mind, it is, that this object, if attainable, is to be reached only by certain legitimate means,—the leading principles of which are no more clearly understood, in the light of to-day, than when the grand system of man, as he is and is to be, was proclaimed and unfolded, long ages ago. To the moral being, the moral law was just as essential then, as it is now, and just as applicable in all its general relations. Progressive, or otherwise, no entangling speculations raise him one tittle above his encompassing responsibilities to the lord of life and master of creation, or aid him to build any enduring kingdom upon what he seems now resolved to call the realities of this world. Even in the physical constitution of nature, he must continue to find many things too high for him, and altogether beyond the limited capacity of his power. Some things, unaccomplished, but yet conceivable, and some, perhaps, as yet inconceivable, he still may become able to do. But he can never float, to any practical purpose, upon the wavering pinions of the air—he cannot ascend the mountain-tops without toil, or return in safety from the uttermost depths of ocean. He may talk of subduing nature, but she controls him—he is strictly subject to all her physical laws and finds no security, except in absolute conformity. A torrent of the mountain sweeps him to destruction,—in defiance of his boasted skill and strength and courage, the proudest bark, that ever rode upon the billow, breaks under him and he sinks into the deep. He has not the slightest conception of the elementary properties of the very wind in which he trusts to waft him all his wealth,—and some unnoticed change in the atmosphere, which is the breathful food of his life,—of the causes and operation of which he really knows nothing,—stretches him upon his bier. He cannot avoid the lightning or resist the whirlwind. Do what he will,—be what he will,—there will still be peril, misjudgment, uncertainty, disappointment, defeat,—his stoutest purposes thwarted, his closest calculations reversed,—he will be the puppet of chance, the slave of circumstances, the subject creature of a power mightier than himself,—there will still be the resistances, the non-conformities, the uncompliant divergencies, the uncontrollable complications of human affairs,—there will still be discordant passions, interests, intelligencies, caprices, hopes and fears,—the failing intellect, the enfeebled frame,—there will still be disease,—there will still be death!

If his thoughts are tempted to pass beyond the routine of his daily toils, perhaps he gazes curiously through a hollow tube, and unnumbered mysterious worlds float within the scope of his projected vision. Of their relations to the globe he inhabits, or to one another, he can form no adequate idea, and he instinctively withdraws from the contemplation of a vast and complex system of the universe, so utterly beyond the compass of his circumscribed imagination, that the effort at its analysis only prostrates his powers. Marvelling, he beholds the fiery messenger of heaven, periodically returning from its range of centuries,—and what proximate idea has ever enlightened his perplexed understanding, as to the mission and uses of this strange and startling visitant of the skies? Under the common blaze of day, when he persuades himself he is acting his highest part amidst the recognized realities of life,—though then, more than ever, he is drawn away from himself, and what he actually is, is confounded and lost,—yet, in the confusion, or the concentration of his mind, he believes, perhaps, in nothing, but that practical, progressive state of society, along whose well-grooved ways and upon whose open, established channels of communication, men are mechanically borne forward to honor and to fortune. But, under the hush of night, he looks into those far depths of unimaginable azure,—he observes the inexpressible loveliness, the unfailing lustre, the unbroken arrangement, the immemorial order and glory of the stars,—not one, broad, diffusive, circumambient atmosphere of daily light,—common to all and, therefore, of no peculiar individual significancy,—and ministering subserviently to his own, amongst the ordinary necessities of mankind,—and upon whose central effulgence he neither cares nor dares to gaze,

—but an infinite, separable, miraculous congregation of rolling worlds, each a beaming witness, indisputable to reason, of something far surpassing the narrow limits of his comprehension, and each an ordained oracle, almost prompting his heart of ignorant pride to whisper to itself—What is man?

This is a serious, and it may seem a sad picture of some of the capacities and prospects of a progressive age,—which, by all the superadded intellectual efforts of long successive generations, it must be admitted, is very imperfectly instructed in regard to heaven above and earth beneath;—but I deem it necessary to be contemplated, and only too suitable to the subject and the times. I summon the Progressive Age, then, and place it at the bar of deliberate and solemn judgment. I ask, what is Progress? and claim its intelligible response. I will be satisfied with no vague, uncertain, sounding generalities, but call for an accurate definition of its nature and its hopes. At least, some appreciable idea of the contemplated voyage is the right of every fellow-passenger, equally interested in the freight, and to be carried forward, whether he will or no, he would gladly learn towards what point of safety, upon the same advancing tide. The object of life, in civilized man alone, or, amongst civilized men associated, is *Good.* What cannot be shown to be good, is generally distinctively evil—and nothing is more likely to be so, than a confused and objectless condition of individual or social existence. Is it no longer to be assumed as certain that there are principles of things, true, eternal, inalienable and unavoidable, and universally applicable to every age and race? Judged by these, if they be admitted, are we to become, intellectually and morally, better or worse? Are we to be more intelligent, more sound, more sober, more just, more honorable, more charitable, more sincere? This is the only test. And, if it cannot be shown that progress is likely to bring about this hopeful reformation, then we may be sure our progress has not taken the shape of advancement,—and we shall be compelled to come to the startling and terrible conclusion, that society, under the modern theory of progress and reality, may be breaking its allegiance to reason, which is the manifestation of truth,—and, without truth, what were this world? what were the universe of God? And yet, though Truth itself will certainly abide, what condition of social existence would that be,—giving no security for life, or property, or freedom,—which, deserting its reverence for that which only is,—this golden, inappreciable, immovable and imperishable *true*,—should yield itself up to the fluttering impulse of the hour? For then, so far from being enlightened, upon any just idea of intelligence,—or safe, upon any probable calculation of stability,—or free, in any rational sense of liberty,—we should have become enslaved to a vague public opinion, which has no substantial, settled, definite, responsible existence,—which sprang up, it knows not how,—is directed by influences, it knows not what, and is rapidly bearing us forward, we know not whither.

But, perhaps, my distinction between an *intellectual* and a *practical* age was unnecessary; and though, upon a superficial glance, they might seem the direct antitheses of each other, yet they may be found, after all, to be mere convertible terms. For, consider that the human being is in his best estate, when his moral attributes coöperate most harmoniously with his intellectual faculties. Could these be perfectly conjoined, according to his order, he would be a perfect being. Divest him of the first, which regulate his relations to society and his Maker, and his mind reverts at once to the contemplation and sordid pursuit of present good. He may build and sow and reap and get gain. He may exercise the keenest insight into all his material aptitudes and necessities and the means of their adaptation and supply. He may fathom not only the depths of physical science, but may speculate within a certain range of intellectual philosophy, and investigate and unfold the subtle principles of human government. So far as his faculties are employed upon the practical pursuits of mankind, he still is merely practical, though he may be eminently intellectual. But if, in regard to moral sense, he hold himself amenable only to the policy of life, his intellectuality, controlled by no reference to immutable truth, will be likely to lead him to mere abstraction,—and abstraction, unless regulated by a just sense of the moral relations of things, is sheer fanaticism. He may seem to himself, then, and to others, to be even a reformer and a philanthropist, and a speculator in the universal, material, external welfare of mankind. The natural quest of the sublimated human mind, working with its own unassisted powers, and dissatisfied with the apparent condition of things, is not after the realization of an excellence in itself, which might be profitable, but for the abstract idea of absolute perfection in human affairs,—for perfect equality,—perfect freedom,—and even, so far as the practice of outward virtue is found requisite to the public interest, for perfect goodness itself,—and yet with no desire prompted by a single just motive. And, so it would be seen, that this speculative intellectualism may be striving after only a seeming positive, which constantly eludes its grasp, and be turning away from only a seeming ideal, which, by gradual assimilation to its nature, might be converted, at length, in its own essence, into a reality of supreme excellence. And so, it would be like the rudderless barque, otherwise fitted to traverse the great Atlantic and Pacific deep, —yet miserably stranded upon the nearest shoal. For, in fact, it would carry into the practical operations of life the very chimera of society, imagined in the mouth of one of his characters, by the universal poet of wisdom—

> I' the commonwealth, I would by contraries
> Execute all things; for no kind of traffic
> Would I admit, no name of magistrate,—
> Letters should not be known; riches, poverty,
> And use of service, none; contract, succession,
> Bourn, bound of land, tilth, vineyard, none;
> No use of metal, corn, or wine, or oil;
> No occupation; all men idle, all,
> And women too.

In a word, such a theorist merely dreams; and his dreams, wearing the semblance only of excellence, are in reality mischievous, instead of beneficial; and the prevalence of his speculations is anything but an encouraging test of the substantial welfare and wisdom of the community. And, accordingly, to such an exemplification of the extravagant impracticabilities of the intellectual era, the wise poet still replies,

> Prythee no more,—thou dost talk nothing to me.

It was a very different glance given by one, whose glances were like the blades of piercing spears, at a social state actually sanctioned by the consenting testimony of all human experience,—by one, who was certainly a very great man (while there were great men) of strong, noble and magnanimous character, and of whose personal virtues, so far as I know or believe, there can be no dispute. It is to be found in the speech of Oliver Cromwell to his second parliament,—couched in his peculiar style of phraseology, and unfolding, within the compass of a hint, the germ of principles always worthy the profoundest consideration.

"And so many of them," says he, "as are peaceably and honestly and quietly disposed to live within the rules of Government, and will be subject to those Gospel rules of obeying magistrates and living under authority,—I reckon no godliness without that circle! Without that spirit, let it pretend what it will, it is diabolical, it is devilish, it is from diabolical spirits, from the depths of Satan's wickedness."

I am detaining you, I know, very much too long, but you will see it is upon a topic susceptible of much more extended and particular treatment, than a lecture permits. Allow me, however, to bring to a close this discussion of social principles, which is so inevitably general, and yet drawn up with no lack of such thoughtful care, as it was in my power to bring to the consideration of a subject, which challenges an interest and attention beyond all others, in its relations to morals and manners and education and government and religion,—in a word, to the structure of society itself and the apparent symptoms of its health or its disorder.

There can be no doubt that the mind of New England has been very much stirred up, in these latter days, and that very great changes have already taken place, in the personal characteristics, as manifested by the expressed opinions and general demeanor of the people. I know that this is called "movement," implying a progressive advancement,—and that it fails not to find many ardent eulogists, in the various departments of public oratory and literature and the press. Those, who are venturesome enough, either to resist or to stand aloof, expose themselves to a good deal of obloquy and ridicule, as men bigotedly and pertinaciously resolved to stay behind the times.

Superfluous lags the veteran on the stage

is the somewhat inconsiderate moral of the modern doctrine. Still, the real question remains, whether these thoughtful persons may not be wisely striving, for their own substantial benefit and that of society, to make good the hold they have upon the solid and permanent shore, while this ungovernable ship, *the times*, has been only buying, at a price, discordant and contrary wind-bags of every treacherous and mischievous witch upon the coast, and then madly putting to sea, amidst these angry and conflicting cross-blasts of

Caurus and Eurus and Argestes loud.

You would not have me say, I know, that amongst

any considerable portion of the better classes, in old-fashioned, sensible, sturdy, worthy, respectable, and consequently respected New England, there was to be seen in morals, rather a convenient formality, than any settled basis of character,—that its former sober and proverbial Yankee inquisitiveness of mind was degenerating into mere flippancy of manners,—that its system of education might be found to prove only a delusion and a snare,—and by growing more technical and wider in its range, it was in danger of becoming little better than the thinnest possible outside burnish,—and that, especially, the lilies of the garden of knowledge were often only very wastefully painted,—that there was really less regard for the great and valuable principles of government, anxiously to be upheld, under all popular institutions, like the pillars of the temple of freedom, than for the management of the state, as a mere engine of political schemers,—and that the fervent faith of the fathers was strangely growing cooled, under the blazing sunshine of an enlightened age, into a more than Laodicean lukewarmness.

And yet, if apart from the manifest improvements in our outward state, there be reason to think, that such are amongst the observable indications of what is now called Progress,—and if, as a consequence it appears, that those, who assume to be our leaders and guides, the organs of public opinion, the controllers of public sentiment, and thus the very contrivers and framers of public action, are of a class, in which such characteristics are more clearly seen, as they are more naturally and easily reached, than the nobler, greater and less easily attainable qualities, which result from high principle and severe self-discipline and a just public requirement,—then to me it seems, that the subject demands the deliberate and undiscouraged devotion of the wisest, best and truest minds amongst us,—and that a steady administration of wholesome truth would profitably take the place of an almost universal spirit of self-laudation. For, seeing our natural faces in such a glass, we straitway forget what manner of men we are. Nor, thus blinded, can any true improvement be made, which is only to be carried forward upon the settled, recognized and universal principles, which spring, like flowers or like weeds, at the very sources of man's moral nature. And this is just as certain, as it is, that humility is the main helper of all virtue and all knowledge, which a conceited, pragmatical and retro-active spirit only obstructs.

I trust I have made no such unprofitable use of my means of observation and reflection, and of the lessons of history and the instructions of religion, as to form any extravagant and indefinite expectations of society. The fruit of the tree of knowledge of good and evil is still as bitter in the mouth of man, as it proved to be, to his original taste. I am quite willing you should understand me to believe that condition of society to be the most healthful and prosperous, in which men really appear superior to one another,—for then we may be sure that some have tasked their better faculties to the utmost,—and that too great uniformity does not, because in the nature of things it cannot indicate the approximation of the entire community to an exalted standard. For, since it is the inevitable lot of humanity to be so preoccupied, that any extraordinary degree of cultivation is generally impracticable, except in those moral attributes, which are within the reach of all, so I do not see how any social state can be really healthful, which exhibits little comparative excellence. Like Mr. Carlyle, I believe in heroes, though (to my misfortune) I never happened to read a word of his pamphlet,—for, without this kind of superiority, popular institutions, which are then deprived of the spur of honorable ambition, which is the breath of their life, soon become corrupt and decay. And what can we say, if the conviction is irresistibly forced upon us, that the dead level of the community, so far from implying the general elevation of the masses, makes only too manifest the unnatural depression of those, who should be the examples and guides of the whole —their conformity to a degraded standard and compliant submission to the base requirements of the crowd.

As society becomes widened and more thoroughly intermingled, under free institutions, there will be found, I fear, a natural tendency to deterioration. The apparently multiplied and diversified objects of life dazzle the imagination of the inexperienced, and draw them out of themselves, and away from the sense of personal responsibility, into the whirling vortex of affairs. The ordinary pursuits of mankind, in great communities, are often in their nature little more than formal and superficial. It is only strong minds, under such circumstances, which will insist upon self-cultivation. Without self-culture, there can be little depth of character, and without this, society soon runs to folly, madness, and dissolution. In a more primitive condition of civilized life, the mind is thrown more directly upon its own resources—the character is more thoroughly formed upon the action of its natural qualities, and is less warped by daily submission to a criterion of opinion, subject to a hundred thousand uncertain influences—and then, if its purposes be good, the man becomes, if not a hero, a statesman, or a sage, at least, in his own degree, a nobler manifestation of his kind. And so, too, great occasions call out great traits. Undoubtedly, war, with all its horrors and woes, often unfolds the noblest, as well as the strongest qualities—courage, honor, hardihood, generosity, self-sacrifice, in man,—the "Ride of the Six Hundred"—the intrepid resolution of Buena Vista,—the rustic heroism of Bunker Hill—in woman, pity, sympathy and a channel wide enough for the unchecked current of all her gushing emotions—she becomes the very genius of patriotism,—of a nobler fortitude, a diviner charity, a sublimer love; and we learn to come up to the sentiment of that "On the shield or with it," of the Spartan mother,—to muse upon the hardly half-told devotion of the women of the Revolution to father, brother, lover, pledged to the embattled service of their country,—or to glow at the story of those angelic ministrations, which have forever blended the idea of relief to the wounded soldier with the name of the sweetest and most piteous songster of the skies.

Certainly, I have not the presumption to imagine, that the views of society in New England, which my own means of observation and reflection have enabled me to suggest, may not be justly subject to modification and correction by the judgment of others. But I cannot help believing, that the idea now so prevalent, that we are being drawn steadily forward in the current of an indefinite progress, is unfounded, as a present fact, even if it be not in general inconsistent with the nature and capacity of man, and therefore, dangerous, in proportion as it is illusory and fallacious. Especially must this be so, if the theory imply any confidence in the advancement of society, which is not absolutely based upon the conscious self-cultivation and responsible moral accountability of its individual members. Logically speaking, society can be in its best estate, only when every individual member of it is performing his own private and public duties, according to his own best means and abilities. Nor will the general good be promoted by compounding for this personal effort, with any loose confidence in a progress, of which we know not the object, the instruments, or the end.

Nor am I willing to subject myself to the misapprehension of presenting a portrayal of the character and tendencies of New England, to its disadvantage, in any other light than by comparison with itself. Whatever opinions I may have been compelled to form in regard to its defects, and making due allowance for all its shortcomings and errors, especially those of a speculative nature, I cannot but reflect, with pride and pleasure, that there is no state or country in the world, where a man is less liable to molestation for his opinions,—which are thus, as it seems to me, most likely to work out their own eventual sanction or condemnation,—or, where he may live in such general freedom and safety. I take the tone of society in New England, however inferior it may be to that of the superior classes, where they are most cultivated and refined in Europe or America, to be yet superior to that of any other population, spread over a region so extensive,—and I choose this standard, therefore, as the basis of such speculations as have occurred to me, in the pursuit of this subject.

It is for the sake of these considerations, that, conceiving the population of New England to be the best criterion I can select, regarding it in all its aspects, without prejudice or favor, it could be hardly too much deplored, should any apparent tendency be exhibited by it to fall away from its ancient high estate. Especially, would it be a subject of profound regret, to see a reckless public sentiment taking the place of whatever true and sound principle gave its former character a superior stability and weight, and a correspondent reputation, upon any just view of the condition of man as an intellectual, moral and accountable being. For it was, unquestionably, the still effective working of the great qualities and characteristics of the founders of New England, which brought out those remarkable traits, developed during the period, which it was my purpose to consider as its *heroic* age,—running through the old French war, and presenting, long subsequently to the Revolution, as worthy a people, influenced and controlled by as numerous a body of able and noble leaders, as was ever seen, in any age of the world.

Perhaps, the very worst thing which could happen to society, in its immediate results, is, to be thoroughly shaken together and settled down to the combined pursuit of the inferior objects of life. What the eventual consequences might prove, Providence only knows. For, by this process, good and evil are inextricably mingled together, and the lightest material is sure to rise to the top. And, under the more ordinary circumstances of life, it is the natural tendency of the minds of men to become belittled, or otherwise, according as the affairs upon which they are individually and exclusively set, are of a grander or a meaner stamp. The immortal mind struggles for the mastery; but thought becomes scattered and confused beyond the possibility of concentration, and men thus lose their hold of those great principles of things, upon which all their present and future interests are dependent. Then it is, that they require great crises in affairs and the storms of the soul, to stir them to their depths and bring them back to the truth. For then, ability is tested, character is weighed, truth is carefully considered, and opinion spread abroad, if not logically sound, returns upon the inventor, instead of going forth, like the down of the thistle,—shall I say, as now? and no man knows, or cares what may become of it. Then, too, men become great, who, in the consciousness of their own weakness, find the elements, the motives and the means of advancing strength. Then, too, society, thus led, can make just progress, because its leaders are really, in their aims and principles and desires, above and beyond the spirit of their age.

It is in vain to ask, what is to be the end of Progress? But I know that society, which cannot take care of itself, and cannot be properly taken care of, except by those whom it educates for that purpose,—can only be wisely directed to any beneficial end by wise and good and true men,—such as every intelligent community should inexorably demand its leading spirits to be. Of such a stamp, with all their faults and failings, was the ancestral stock of New England, and I need not offer evidence to convince you, that the basis of that character, upon which the reputation of New England really rests, was formed long, very long before our own day. And, although there are inevitable points of difference between the condition of our ancestors and our own, I know that no salutary advancement can be made, in whatever constitutes the substantial welfare of life, without the better personal qualities which they exhibited, without the honest motives which prompted their conduct, without the learning which they honored and the virtues which they reverenced. But, amidst all our growing faults, I believe there are still the elements of great excellence left in New England. I am no believer in general intellectual degeneracy. The unextinguished mind of man, through every age of darkness, has vindicated his immortal capacity and been the manifest witness of God.

The future is not ours,—but I can conceive of causes, which would tend to concentrate and revive, once more, what I hope is the essentially sound mind of New England. And we might then have a progress, fitted to effect a reformation, if possible, not to be reformed,—to fix high principle,—to develop the faculties,—to raise the character,—and relieve it of frivolities and formalities and insincerities—to draw the intellectual being away from erroneous and unprofitable and degrading channels of investigation, where only it creeps which ought to soar—to allure it to philosophy, rather than speculation—to induce it to rise on wings of beaming light, which remain folded or unfolded as we choose, above the surface of things, and so gain impulse to go sounding down to the depths of thought, the elements of government, the foundation of morals, the reasonableness of religion,—to turn it away from the spirit of chicanery and the miserable self-delusions, which infect modern society—so that it may buy the truth and sell it not,—that is, hold it in possession, like an heir-loom of glory, and part with it at no price,—to bring the mind safely back from its empty wanderings into inexplorable space, and teach the man to devote his powers to that world of duties and wants, follies and errors, temptations and trials,—the microcosm of himself. And we,—the descendants of the Pilgrims and the Puritans, who, according to their light, had views of extraordinary clearness, and yet perhaps saw not all things,—let us devoutly cherish our trust in the prevalence of such glorious progress as this, promoted by sincere hearts and perpetuated in endless peace,—the very name of which, one of the chiefest orators of antiquity pronounced so sweet—*Et nomen pacis dulce et ipsa res salutaris.*

And yet, if Providence shall have determined otherwise,—still let us trust that, in some fiercer domestic struggle, it may be, to which all states and nations are only too subject, or in some fairer exercise of conflict with a foreign foe, we should find our honored and beloved New England brought back more steadily to the just balance of her inherent character,—yet having her divines, her orators, her scholars, her soldiers, her patriots, her citizens like those of old,—and, in the glowing language of our lyric poet, whose laurels, wreathed upon his brow by your own noble State, are still the inherited honors of her soil,—yet counting, amongst her choicest jewels, the true successors of those, to whose memory the mind instinctively reverts, in every hour of darkness and public perplexity—

> Men, who swayed senates with a statesman's soul,
> And looked on armies with a leader's eye.

THE USES AND ABUSES

OF

THE DAILY PRESS.

THE subject of my Lecture this evening, will be "The Daily Press." An extraordinary theme of discussion, perhaps you will say, this general object of daily interest, common as the air, the companion of our firesides and of all our resorts of business or pleasure; suited, in its multiplied manifestations, to our tastes, our habits, our pursuits, our recreations,—in fact, to all the diversified elements of the human mind, and become, at last, an absolute necessity of life. I am not aware, that anybody before has made this miscellaneous text-book of popular literature the topic of a philosophical lecture. But I think you will see, that the very universality, which it claims, challenges your closest consideration of its titles to regard; and that an honest investigation of the characteristics, the merits, the deficiencies, the powers, and the obligations of anything, upon which you are really so dependent, ought to afford the materials and the motives for your profoundest interest.

"We read newspapers, it is true," you reply,—"they serve the momentary purpose of their production and circulation; they bear us along with them, abreast of the rapid flood of passing events; they give us our morning subjects of discussion, and wipe the misty cobwebs of dreamland out of our opening eyes; they afford the materials of our evening solace, and we drop them with our final yawn, as we sink into the embraces of nature's sweet restorer; we glance through their columns, for casual and temporary amusement,—really, we seldom discover anything, which dwells very seriously upon the mind; what they contain makes, after all, but a very slight impression; in a moment, we should be at a loss to recall anything which met our eyes; we fling them aside with indifference, though, in truth, we should miss them absent,—and who cares, afterwards, for an old newspaper?"

It is true, really, that there was nothing to-day,—to-morrow, perhaps, there will be something, to hear or to tell, for these modern Athenians, always pursuing, often balked, but never turned aside, from their anxious quest after some new thing. So far, in fact, as you have acquired any information of serious and personal interest,—anything, which intimately concerns the chief ends and high-reaching capacities of man's rational life and the perfection of his character, the impression of successive days will prove, probably, quite as evanescent. What the reader has actually learned, towards the advancement of his intellectual and moral nature,—if, in these days of wandering thought and confused motive, such an object is yet within the range of telescopic vision—his acquisitions, in this behalf, may have been little better than a blank. He may have passed, in daily review, perhaps, successive and repeating columns of these circumambulatory oracles of modern society, to the framing and unfolding of whose winged responses went so many busy fingers and still busier brains—and as he turns aside from the inspection, what distinct idea remains in his mind, of that rapid succession of incident, and of those intermittent flashes of speculation, which played rather upon his eye, than ranged themselves intelligibly before his understanding? The interest was transient, and it is gone. The gathered results of his eager enquiry after knowledge, where are they to-morrow? Where are they today? The listless hour, which they occupied, took with it its vague impressions,

> Making them momentary as a sound,
> Swift as a shadow, short as any dream,
> Brief as the lightning in the collied night,
> That in a spleen unfolds both heaven and earth,
> And ere a man hath power to say, Behold!
> The jaws of darkness do devour it up.

Were the newspaper really *old*, it might indeed be estimated at sterling value. What a host of reviving memories the aspect of one of those dingy sheets of another day inspires! No effort of merely human intellect could now avail to keep pace with the ever-moving and constantly intermingling squadrons of the modern press, as, file by file, they wheel into the field of sight and march with the ever moving hours! But, what touching, what affecting, what pictorial associations cluster around their periodical advent, when dailies were not, but the primitive weekly sheet, with its well-considered summary of life's distant incident, and its homebred speculations, colored with the sober hues of thoughtful interest, made its eventful evening appearance, at the secluded village or the provincial town!

> He comes, the herald of a noisy world,
> News from all nations lumbering at his back—

The hardy postman, perhaps, has brought it through drifting snows,—or the stony street has echoed to the wheels of the long-expected stage-coach,—and now, the welcome budget is just at hand! Close fast the shutters, and let the eager circle around the cheerful fireside, shut out, for a long, long week, from much intercourse with the remoter world, listen to all, which has stirred the hearts and affected the minds, and moulded the fortunes of men and cities, within the round of our domestic or national sympathies,—or, dwell, with all the vivid instincts of a wondering magination, upon distant news, which, for weary months, has been laboring towards us from farthest Ind,—

Damascus, or Morocco, or Trebizond.

It is possible, that the antiquated perceptions of our predecessors may have been occupied, in the meantime, with reading quite as profitable and instructive; that, during the intervals of this intellectual communication with the outer world, they may have found employment for the mind, calculated to enchain and reward the attention,—that what they read or reflected informed the judgment, instead of scattering the thoughts, satisfying the mind with a glance, flitting over its unstamped surface, like successive shadows, neither imparting strength, nor educing its own energies; and so rendering it really wavering and inefficient in action, and incapable of the nobler and hardier elements of its condition and being.

And what would we not gladly give for *some* old newspapers, which suggest themselves, as amongst the possibilities of the imagination? Bring us in, if you please, a file of the "Crusader." I should like to look over again the telegraphic report of that stirring sermon of Peter the Hermit, which raised Europe out of itself, and sent the flower and chivalry and the yeomanry of Christendom, for a cause of the heart, if not of the understanding, to do battle and perish, piously and thankfully, on the burning plains of Syria. Let us read, as they transpired, the events of that pictured narrative, which has intermingled with the tissue of the world's history one broidered filament of golden romance, lasting as its annals, and, now and forever, twining itself inextricably around all the social relations of civilized life. What price would be too dear, for an "Independent Press," for example, or the "Daily Clarion," of the period, proclaiming, in trumpet-tones, its denunciations of that brutal Henry of England, who made a shambles of his loves,—or of his still bloodier daughter, who slew the innocent for their faith? Or, shall we call for the Galignani, of three hundred years ago, and muse upon minuter details than glow, even on Sully's fascinating page, of the early adversities and heroic struggles of that other Henry,—the conqueror of Ivry and bestower of the Edict of Nantes—of adversities borne like a man who was more than a king,—of his final triumph,—of his heavy doom, "fatal to liberty,"—fatal to all which that age could grant to the progress of freedom. Let our hearts glow, as we welcome, over the misty mountain's top, the dawnings of a brighter day, foretokening a purer faith. Let our zeal kindle to resist the machinations of the Medici, that bigoted and cruel race. How can we help a vow of vengeance, as we read of murder dabbling the silver hairs of the good Coligni with his blood? Let us recall the massacre of St. Bartholomew, in the guilt of its instant horrors, unparalleled, says the French historian, by equal barbarity, in all antiquity or the annals of the world. We have heard their tale,—let us speed, on the errand of mercy, to the inmost fastnesses and retreats of the persecuted Vaudois, or cheer the indignant message of stout, magnanimous Cromwell, remonstrating, with words that spoke of flame and thunder and the sword, against Superstition, guilty of the blood of—

——— slaughtered saints, whose bones
Lie scattered on the Alpine mountains cold!

Or, what should we say to the "Puritan Recorder" of 1620, faintly portraying the inexpressible emotions of Carver and Bradford and Brewster and Standish and the rest,—as they launched upon the scarcely traversed ocean of their pilgrimage, to brave the commingled yet conflicting elements of the coming winter and the unknown sea,—and left, with lingering looks, the home of their human affections, that they might peacefully commune, in the exile of a savage land, with the dearer home of their souls!

And yet, who would care to see all the glittering blazonry of human history sobered down by the homely daub of utilitarian philosophy, or reduced within the petty compass of a pen-and-ink sketch? Who would wish, that all the sacred and tender mysteries of life should be accurately sounded and surveyed and mapped out, before his eyes,—and every gleaming headland, on the vast ocean of time, taken in its bearings and distances, with the clear and sober certainty of geometrical analysis? I rejoice that there is yet something uncertain, secret, mysterious, indefinable, grand—altogether out of the scope of the peering researches and shallow philosophy and hasty, unreflecting speculations of the day. I rejoice that there are yet left gaps and fissures, along the royal highway of Time, beyond all engineering art to level and subdue,—which only Imagination can fill up with her own deepening colors, and people with forms and shapes and fancies of her own legitimate creation. It may be the aim and hope of the Present, to bring down much which constitutes the grace, and grandeur and beauty of the world to its own criterion of well-investigated and well-defined mediocrity. But behind us, in the Past, are the mountains which cannot be touched. Between them lie sweet, mysterious valleys, practicable only to their enfranchised denizens, and never to be explored by the impertinent aggressions of modern curiosity,—within the recesses of whose shadowy forests forever sits the nymph, yet prophetic by the side of her whispering fountain, and the sage, whose lessons of the past are now and ever will be the irreversible wisdom of life.

But what shall we say to this grasping Present? Shall it lift the veil, which has hitherto shrouded the decencies and imparted some wholesome awe to the proprieties and dignities of nature? Shall it creep forward and forward, with noiseless step, until it becomes exaggerated into a power multiform, inquisitive and irresponsible,—entering, like the plague of Egypt, into our bed-chambers and our ovens and kneading-troughs,—before whose ominous advances modesty shrinks away and virtue is appalled, and under whose cold, scrutinizing eye vice is publicly paraded, until the flush of detected shame fades from her callous cheek,—and our half-formed aspirations for good and the cherished affections of our lives, and the thoughts we would not reveal to a brother and whisper in no audible tones to our own hearts,– shall they be remorselessly rifled from our breasts and flung, sensitive and palpitating, into the common mart, to be trampled over by the inconsiderate and jeering throng?

Do I object, therefore, to the freedom of the press? I protest only against its mismanagement. If it has its value, it has also its defects. I object only to its license, its incompetence, its shallowness, its impertinence, its venality. I urge only the prevalence of those evils, in the reformation of which, those who control it and those who are controlled by it have a common cause. It is the idlest cant in the world, this talk which it sometimes employs, about shackling its freedom. It can be restrained, in this land of liberty, only by its own self-respect and a decent observance of the settled sentiments of mankind. I know of no reason, why freedom of opinion should not be indulged, in a fair discussion of its claims to public confidence and regard. The only real danger to the press is, that it will grow too autocratic in the excess of its own pampered liberty. I know how little one earnest tongue can do against the incessant murmurs of its ten thousand mouths. But I am conscious of no vague dread of a power, not always wisely and justly administered; and besides, I believe that the ablest and soundest conductors of the press are only too conscious of such deficiencies and necessities, as I might feel it within my province to point out.

One of the early governors of Virginia once stated the fact, as a matter of exultation, that there was not a newspaper in the entire territory under his administration; and an eminent member of Congress, from the same State, more recently took occasion to thank God, that nothing of the sort could be found in his district. He had observed, perhaps, how potent an instrument it had become for good, or for evil,—irresistible in its combined energies, when it maintained the right, and before which no individual strength, or virtue or genius could stand, when it chose, or stumbled upon the wrong. His mind, undoubtedly, had looked upon the subject only in its least flattering aspects. I fear I too shall have to take some unfavorable views of the present administration of the press;

but, in speaking of its evils, my purpose is only to see how it may best be made instrumental to the public good and its own. I can conceive of a state of public sentiment, which would demand a higher tone, and would reward the application of nobler powers, than are usually bestowed upon the conduct of the journals of the times. In a country like this, the Press,—more than its Legislatures,—should be in the hands of its most enlightened and worthiest citizens. Instead of making it a mere record of passing events, or a mere channel of time-serving speculations upon trivial and temporary affairs,—or a mere pander to popular appetite, corrupting the public and corrupting itself,—would its conductors take into consideration sometimes the object of raising, as well as merely entertaining the public mind, what a glorious field of usefulness might be opened within the sphere of their already incalculable influence! Surely, I do not mean to allege, that there are not newspapers, and many, which are conducted with more or less reference to a principle so generous and beneficent. But who will deny, that there is a mighty swarm besides, issued solely upon the selfish consideration of pecuniary advantage,—ready to tamper with any principle,—prompt to listen to any scandal, glad to sell mischief and abuse by the square,—eager to bargain, either to apply or withhold a venal praise? Who, that has examined this subject, must not sorrowfully admit, that, instead of using their means of usefulness to its appropriate end, they have tended, in many ways, to the manifest corruption of the popular mind? That they have demeaned public sentiment, diluted public taste, weakened public judgment? And that, amongst not the least of the evils, to which they have subjected society, they have substituted themselves, thus reduced in character and aim, for higher and better sources of knowledge; and have accustomed us to rely upon the crude and flimsy and irresponsible speculations of a veiled and, therefore, mysteriously effective agency, for the old, sound, manly sense of the individual citizen, self-dependent and, therefore, self-reliant, who exercised himself in wholesome investigation and reflection, and came to his honest and satisfactory conclusions, by a process of hard thought? But who will take the trouble of thinking, when the newspaper editor is paid, for doing this tedious business in his behalf? And thus the man is taken away from the exercise of his own powers; he learns to distrust a judgment, which he does not use; he becomes the puppet of others, of perhaps, no higher qualifications than himself, who play with his opinions, loosen the hold of his social and personal obligations, gradually modify his thoughts, mould his sentiments, form his character,—leave him not a thinking, but an artificial and a superficial man,—and too often convert him into one of those feeble and wavering creatures, common enough in our day, who are swayed by the weakest impulses and are insensible of the highest duties of manhood and citizenship and religion itself.

If there be any soundness in the views thus indicated, and if correspondent changes only too obvious have come over the face of society, I am compelled to believe, that the main cause will be found, in the good-natured sufferance of the public towards the least respectable portion of the daily press. And, for my own part, I hesitate not to avow, that I would sooner rely, for a sound judgment upon men and manners and things, on the plain, thinking, well-schooled philosopher of nature, amidst her woods and fields, in the dimmest valley of the land,—where the morning radiance of the daily press scarcely sheds its pervading beams,—but another gospel, of benigner light, opens and instructs his understanding,—than upon the opinions of many of those, with whom you and I are most conversant in the common walks and intercourse of our lives,—the busiest men in the active pursuits of the world, who read all the newspapers,—that intermingled mass of eager, moving, wavering, puzzled beings, called society of to-day, men of unsettled thoughts and indecisive minds,—who live in a blaze which serves only to dazzle and bewilder them, who learn little enough at any fountain-head of true and sober knowledge, but drink intoxicating draughts from every shallow rivulet, which trickles or stagnates on their way.

I know that all this may seem to some little better than rank heresy to the spirit of the age and its main instruments of thought. But I claim, that the great body of the newspapers of the day, as they are generally conducted, do not fairly meet the assumed demands and necessities of the times. If they are to be read as mere matters of amusement, and to occupy only our idle hours, if such hours are to be found, or ought to be found, in this modern busy, bustling world of ever-existing and constantly-growing responsibilities,—even here there is a high duty devolving upon them, to restrain their present tendency, wilfully or carelessly to mislead and debauch the public mind. If the age be really unsound and insincere, given over to frivolity, devout only in its material longings, impatient of truth, listening only with eager interest to preachers of smooth things,—then, nothing can be so effectual, as a corrupt and subservient press, to foster its unspiritual habitudes, and to pander profitably to appetites, which grow by what they feed on,—until the unwholesome leaven has finally worked itself into all the constituent elements of the incorporated mass,—and cause and consequence begin to act interchangeably upon each other, and the things which once were real become to us little better than shadows, and those which we once sought for our blessings are now our bane, and the names of former glory are but a mockery and a reproach, and virtue, truth, honor and religion,—the dignity of learning and the incitements to manly enterprise,—the grace, the charm and the ornament of life,—the aims, the ends and the means of knowledge,—all sink together into one common abyss of degradation, ignominy and ruin.

But, on the other hand, let us soberly inquire if the spiritual hopes of mankind, like doves flocking to their windows, are now entitled to rest their weary feet upon the aspiring edifice of human improvement? Have the new builders of this temple of Progress presented it to our eyes, truly a stable, magnificent and imposing sanctuary, for the refuge of burdened and anxious and despondent thought, fit to be the elect cathedral of a true spiritual worship? In clearing away the accumulated rubbish of ages, from every vaulted crypt, weakening nothing in the solid foundation of the admirable structure, have they brought only more prominently forward the venerable tombs of the good and great, who lie beneath, where alternate light and shadow touch them with an intermingling harmony of glory and gloom? Will what they have affixed superincumbent, upon the uprising and stately pile, be likely to prove only a buttress of strength,—so that every fretted pinnacle and stalwart tower and soaring spire, shall seem growing day by day, only nearer to the skies? Are we sure that all within the hallowed precincts is decent and fraternal and just and wise, as truly becomes the completer framework of the social system of an advancing age? Is it certain that no trivial, faithless and mocking spirit pervades the assembled multitude, desecrating the temple, while it enfeebles and degrades their own hearts? Does no self-seeking and subservient idol of an insane worship, fashioned by men's hands, clothed with vanity and crowned with lies, sit grinning an empty approval, behind the altar of their devotion? In a word, does the substantial progress of life consist, not in the mere externals of society,—not in those walls and ships and houses,—which the old Greek poet, three thousand years ago, affirmed could never constitute a state,—looking deeply into the capacities and necessities of our nature, and observing those true signs of mental and moral development, which do constitute greatness or its opposite?

For, if the true foundation of Progress be not laid in whatever makes up the grand sum of substantial superiority in man, and shows him a nobler, higher, better and happier being than before,—more able, intellectually, so far as intellect avails, to demonstrate the great problem of life,—more earnest, morally, as well he may be, to apply the means of existence to their legitimate ends,—if truth, that first indispensable element of all substantial excellence, has failed to become the rule of life, and the law of its ordinary action,—and justice has not, at length, been able to remove that obnoxious and blinding fillet from before her eyes, and not yet merit wins its due reward, nor goodness seems as lovely as it is, —if these, and other correspondent indications, be not amongst the observable signs of a (so-called) advancing age,—how can we style that *progress*, which exhibits only a more striking failure to conform to the very fundamental principles of our being? For if society be not thus seen moving—if not with one spontaneous and general consent of action,—yet, its effective battalions in advance, its music and banners to the front, its sentinels falling, one by one, into rank, and gradually drawing every distant outpost into the line of the forward march, together with the whole promiscuous multitude of the hangers-on and hangers-back of the upbreaking and victorious camp, —if society be not thus visibly moving towards the outer boundary (if boundary be conceded) of the intellectual and moral advancement of the race,—then, I beg to suggest the conclusion, as one of instant and unavoidable application,—that the scouts, skirmishers and pioneers, who are to clear the way of conquest, should themselves be more true,—that the newspaper press itself, the common and necessary instrument adapted to promote the public improvement and its information, upon points entering into all the vast and indefinable relations of public and private life, should become more consonant with the hopes of the leading minds of the nation, and should afford such instruction upon our weightiest interests, as every rational anticipation of a higher condition of social intellect and moral sensibility so imperatively demands.

And it may be, after all, that no ungenerous sketch of the elements of our social characteristics may find some justification in a liberal estimate of the aspects and tendencies of the times. It does not necessarily follow, I hope, that knowledge grows weaker, as it becomes diffused. I sincerely trust, that the limited degree of general enlightenment, which the great mass of mankind is actually able to compass,—not certainly complete, or perfect, or universal, but preclusively confined very much within the range of the ordinary necessities and powers and the absolute requirements of life,—should tend rather to lower than to raise the standard of human knowledge, and should operate to the actual discouragement of our higher faculties and capacities of attainment, by the incessant, multiplied and combined competitions of those of an inferior grade. It may not be a necessary result of the very constitution of our nature, that the broader diffusion of a certain generally-attainable amount of knowledge, more or less definite or profound, should have the effect to render the absolute and positive fund of human information and learning and thought,—all to be acquired and cultivated and wrought out only by assiduous labor, or grasped only by exalted genius, severally in the untiring application of his own specific faculties, by the statesman, the scholar, the philosopher and the poet,—less really available to the substantial elevation of the species,—of man as man, each having a common interest in the sum of good, and each catching some reflected glow from the constellated firmament of his brotherhood, who have "rejoined the stars,"—and that a result so unhappy should be brought about by a constant and frittering process of intellectual amalgamation,—so that the relations become really confused between the half-thinker or shallow thinker, and the mind gifted and inspired to teach,—and no longer one star seems to differ from another star in brightness; but the misty orb, on the outer verge of the distant horizon, reveals its twinkling beams, as beneficently and resplendently beautiful, to the common apprehension, as the glory of the upper host of heaven, which magnificently shine, and shine, and forever shine on,—and charlatans, sciolists and smatterers obtain the mastery of affairs, and vain and empty pretension becomes the rule and standard of life; and they, who yield a bewildered deference to this degraded and degrading dominion, forfeit at once the motive, the reason and the example for the attainment of superior excellence. But the theory I would suggest gains some force from the proposition,—that, since correct habits and aptitudes of thought, upon speculative subjects always, and upon matters of practice, as a general rule, can be formed only by the few, who have opportunities, instead of the many, who are immersed in their individual affairs,—and, since sound and accurate thinkers are as rare as great men, and the list of those whom we could name, amongst the perfectly reliable masters of the mind and its attributes, would be found exceedingly limited in our own day,—it must be, that the multitudes of distinguished personages, whom the newspaper press is continually offering to our admiration, are in fact great, rather as multiples of each other, and only by the combined force of their aggregated powers, than upon the basis of any individual claim to the general deference and respect.

And when we reflect upon the extraordinary development, energy and brilliancy of the human intellect, as displayed in the pursuits of science, philosophy, literature and arms, during the first half of the present century, to go no further back, and consider that scarcely a preëminent living teacher of the human mind, so far as I am aware, can be pointed out, to meet the present wants and aspirations of an advancing age, and to save it from very trivial tendencies and many miserable delusions, degrading enough for a period absolutely deficient in newspapers,—when, certainly, within the circle of literature, meaning no derogation to the merits of two or three eminent names, there is no great poet or novelist, of the order known to that earlier era, to offer us, and so to be accepted, as if of divine inspiration,—the purer and sweeter and nobler pictures of life,—to animate us with exalted sentiments, as if an oracle had breathed its spirit to mingle with the inner longings of the soul, to stimulate and enchant the fancy, and to fill the imagination with charming pictures, which almost satisfied and controlled its capacities, and glittering as the frost-work on every pendent bough, which the sunlight of this brilliant wintry day has invested with a more than fairy lustre, throughout the ample area of Nature's magnificent temple;—when we conceive, that an enduring and desperate warfare, convulsing the mightiest states of Europe, reversing the speculative doctrines of centuries, and the historical, traditional and legendary prejudices of nations, and involving, probably, the future destinies of Christendom,—that this warfare has awakened the dormant faculties of no leading statesman, biding his time and fitted for the time, and, strangest of all, has brought forward no unquestionable hero, no recognized king of men,—to the gaze of an expectant and admiring world,—it must give us some pause, as to the unsettled problem, of the still advancing progress, or the receding intellectual pretensions of the age.

In the exercise of such judgment as I am able to apply to this knotty question, I am compelled to believe, upon evidence, that there is in fact some apparent deficiency, the just ascertainment of which ought to stagger the overweening intellectual estimate, at present so prevalent amongst us. But is there not something, after all, in the theory I have imperfectly proposed,—and is not the newspaper press really responsible for a social mischief, seriously demanding the public attention and claiming its own reformation, at the hazard of public distrust, involving its eventual contempt? Ah, if I am to pay a devout worship, I ask no idols of wood or stone, or things, which I can trample upon and destroy, but give me gods! Give me something, which in the consciousness of my own nature I acknowledge as higher than I, and to which I tender the supreme homage of my soul, because of its inherent essence of superior virtue! My mind revolts from the adoration of things of brass and clay! And is not this, too often the senseless and fruitless worship, which this self-constituted image-maker of the Press, day by day, sets up?

If, as the poet says (and well the poet knew) *excellence is the eternal food of envy*, this may account sufficiently for that spirit of detraction, which too often leads the Press flippantly to arraign and improvidently to misjudge men of more than common mark,—to undervalue their abilities, to slur over their virtues, to gloat at the discovery of their failings, to molest their lives and despoil even their graves of the privileged sanctity of repose. But, since true greatness defies every ordeal, and we may, therefore, let this pass, what shall we say to a practice still more vicious, and hostile to whatever is sound and wholesome in the constitution of society—which, by no warrant, except that authoritative plural number,—that sovereign "We,"—which presupposes editors and kings to represent the voice of the people, which is the voice of God,—gives out delusive oracles, which have the eventual influence to mislead, though they may seem to find little immediate response in the popular breast? For thus it is they are so ready to lavish printed praises upon those, who are really unfitted for public distinction; to attribute superlative merit to very ordinary men; to make heroes and geniuses out of very flimsy, commonplace material; to create such hosts of human wonders, that the order of nature is reversed and exceptions become the marvels,—to replenish the golden fountain of eloquence out of the mouth of every petty politician,—although profane history, certainly, has sent us down but two preeminent names of the orators of all antiquity, and their genius trained by the laborious efforts of a life, fostering and developing nature,—and one slight page might easily hold all who have come after them;—and, though the list of the great poets of the world scarcely gives one, for a century, during the period of its reliable secular history, to claim the very harp-strings of the master of all song, for every pretty fluttering warbler, fitted perhaps to regale us with the passing melodies of the hour,—to set a thousand scribbling men and women temporarily beside—

—— the few, the immortal names,
Which were not born to die,—

when those who owned the names, until they were fairly dead in the body no medicinal fame often thought of embalming,—to laud private and common virtues, and so insult society, as if these were actually its anomalies and phenomena,—to blazon charity, whose modesty is her merit, and who is a virtue only when her face is veiled,—to descend, for the objects of our exalted admiration into the daily round of our ordinary pursuits,—to constitute half our Dogberries Solons and militia-men gods of war,—and even to personify in print Policeman X—to flatter publicly, for common duties properly performed, the well-disposed director of the train, the attentive clerk of the steam-boat, the obliging assistant at the hotel, the disinterested purveyor of the public feast,—instead of a meek and quiet spirit, to stir up another, which is conventional, superficial, cockneyish, pert and blustering,—to foster idle vanity and small conceit,—to stimulate ill-founded ambitions,—to create petty jealousies,—to engender mortifications and bad blood,—to stagger and discourage good sense,—to injure unpretending merit and genuine desert, which scorn to employ the unworthy arts, of which they are thus indirectly the victims,—to squander vapid eulogies, which seek out and minister to, if they do not actually create, a vitiated public sentiment, but never to dig up concealed gold, laboriously and generously, and hold it forth, for the worth of the pure metal, and challenge for it its due value,—to render, in a word, their praise and their censure, which, if sparingly used, would be and ought to be valuable, equally worthless to a just mind, because reckless and indiscriminating,—to pervert the truth of nature, by the creation of a petty standard of public estimation, and thus, to confute and confound the genuine distinctions between excellence and inferiority,—good and ill,—upon which the just balance of the whole economy of life, and all that is worth a moment's thought, is solely dependent,—and so, to infect with fatal disorders the very heart and soul of our ordinary being. And I cannot think the picture has been too darkly colored, since it is easy to see how rapidly society may be lowered by the operation of such causes. I do not really believe, that the human mind, in its inherent attributes and characteristics, has absolutely dwindled in our day, as the criterion of the newspapers might lead us to apprehend,—but I do think, that a false and vicious standard of things, rapidly taking precedence of the true, and resulting, I fear, from a depreciated moral sense, has tended very much to the obscurity of our mental vision,—just as he, who goes abroad, under the loveliness of the shining night, and holds a farthing candle to his eyes, shall see nothing of the eternal blue above, or of the enduring lustre of the ever-rolling stars.

From such a condition of things as I have attributed to, perhaps, the most popular portion of the Press, to gossip and scandal the step is easy,—until little real regard is paid, by newspapers of even much higher pretensions, to that truth which is the life-blood of all civilized society, or that decency which is its necessary mantle. So that we live abroad, instead of at home, which is the sole fountain-head of all reliable virtue, and the privacy of life is converted into an open spectacle,—and details, in which our firesides, if we respect them, can have no share, and malicious discussions of character, such as no private assembly of reputable men and women would countenance, are daily presented in print, for the amusement and to the peril of the injudicious and unthinking. And we may justly fear, that the best-conducted portion of the press is becoming only too careless in regard to the responsibilities of publication, and, that,—separating and leaving off two of the important elements in the apostle's triply-conjoined definition of charity,—of theirs it can only be said, and that in more senses than one—"It believeth all things."

But a newspaper, in order to be useful, or even to retain the semblance of its wonted authority, must be careful not to come down to the momentary and fluctuating impressions of the populace. In some sense, if it have any value for its character, it is constituted an arbiter and a judge between the Truth and its constant liability to factious or interested popular perversion. As a mere vehicle for the diffusion of general intelligence, it should exercise a judgment and forbearance, regulated by some just standard of true public utility. It should present us only with such articles of information, as it behoves the public to know,—not seeking merely to gratify a prurient curiosity, but affording whatever may be valuable and useful to men and women, who have serious business in the world to perform, or who require to be refreshed and invigorated by innocent amusement. And, above all, it should make only those persons the subjects of public comment, who are really public property,—such as candidates for office, or those who come before the world voluntarily, as literary or professional men, who ought to expect to be properly discussed, and a thorough investigation of whose claims is the public right and enures to the general benefit.

Indeed, in a condition of society devoted so thoroughly to this description of reading, as a substitute for books, and which is fast taking the place of books of any sterling value, the profession of an editor, however lightly it is often undertaken, seems to me a charge of very high responsibility. Certainly, in a country of free institutions, the daily questions arising in the science of politics,—which, although a little distorted in its practical operation, is but another name for public morals,—require the application of abilities of no common order; and, unless the trumpet is to give an uncertain sound, demand a keenness of susceptibility to the motives and obligations of duty, to be found only in the complete organization of the head and heart of a whole man. That he, who undertakes to instruct others, should be himself a person of sound education, I care not how acquired, would be only a truism, if the theory were not so frequently contradicted in practice. And if the mind of him, who addresses us under so many interesting aspects, shall have been substantially trained by the reason, if not the rules of logic,—if he has been fortunate and diligent enough to have gathered up the treasures of a broad general information,—if he has accustomed himself to the exercise of a rapid analytical faculty,—if he enjoy the blessings of stability of purpose, conscientiousness, prudence, forethought and forbearance, possess the rare ability to see a question in all its relations, the sagacity to discover and boldness enough to tell the wholesome truth,—he would then be such an editor, as we would gladly see at the head of more of the newspapers, now disseminated so widely over the surface of our common country. Indeed, I know of nothing more refreshing, in our times, than to take up unexpectedly a sterling newspaper,—and such there are,—which has the ring of the true metal about it,—neither conventional nor qualified, nor looking after momentary applause,—not appearing before our eyes, tricked out in harlequin garments of opinion, patched over with the shreds and tatters of real or supposed popular prejudice,—but cheering us with the honest sentiments of one, who does not forget he is a man, though an editor,—who looks over society with a just purpose, seeing its wants, rebuking its errors, encouraging its better impulses,—not waiting to see which way the current will eventually move, and so holding back for a favorable moment to jump upon the top of the flowing tide, under the weak fear of losing some unsteady and often worthless patronage, —but meeting and taking the responsibility,—really digging for the truth, which is the great public concern, as for hid treasures,—in the discharge of his proper duties of investigation and reflection, really leading, because he has thought, instead of following the public mind,—which thinks, too, but not always correctly upon its first impulse,—and thus, upon a substantial basis, meriting, and consequently, in one satisfactory shape or another, winning his due reward.

I know well enough that there are newspapers of a high and improving stamp amongst us. Perhaps, the popular demand for those of a higher grade has not yet fully warranted that general division of labor, which collects the available talent of many, each in his specific sphere of usefulness, for the instruction and entertainment of the multitude, and thus renders the journals of the old world so much superior to our own. Certainly, no one person can be expected to know everything. But, on the other hand, absolute ignorance on the part of editors, in regard to the common topics of intellectual society, is an offence, culpable because implying presumption, and because it is directly prejudicial to the cause of human improvement. And, no doubt, the reader sometimes thinks it a serious abuse, when the editors do not seem to know how often a good story, or a good joke has been produced before, and impute to the sailor or the Hibernian of to-day jests and blunders, much older than those found in the facetious, but somewhat familiar writings of the late Mr. Miller,—such as the Greeks and Romans laughed at, many centuries ago, and which amused our boyhood,—and still more, when they bring forward the very common-places of literature, as if they were fresh contributions to the fund of good learning,—treating us over again, for new, with the high sentiment and generous thought, sparkling like jewels on the golden pages of the masters of mere English letters and philosophy,—which they imagine they have thus discovered, though others have dug them out often and long before,—and so, by their mode of reproducing other men's creations, not only rob them of their just praise, but, thus checking invention, throw positive obstacles in the way of human progress and improvement.

But above all others, there is one field of discussion, upon which newspapers, now-a-days, have somewhat arrogantly entered, in the labor of which they have shown, to a marked degree, their own inefficiency in the ordinary arts of cultivation, and have well nigh converted the fair domain of the republic of letters into an unwholesome wilderness of worthless and noxious weeds. I think they are responsible for it, in an eminent degree, and the fact shows how really disqualified newspaper editors often are for the office of literary critics. I will give them the credit of sometimes admitting, that they are not themselves very well versed in such matters, and of pleading, that the necessities of their position preclude them from the proper consideration of subjects, so essential to the welfare of all intelligent and cultivated society. But then, the wonder grows, with what hope of generous service to a noble cause, against that stalking giant of Error, always advancing to defy the armies of Truth,—they put on harness which they have not proved,—and upon what theory of moral accountability, they yield up their means of influence, if not their judgment and duty, to interested and often incompetent parties, who, for the most selfish ends, mislead and abuse the public mind and inflict infinite injury upon the cause of a healthy and serviceable literature. I do not mean to assert, that an entirely accurate knowledge of the technical canons of criticism, however useful,—and a mind stored with all the diversified accomplishments of elegant scholarship, and a memory, furnished, like a well-ordered battery, with all the bristling armament of attack and defence,—though of the utmost service, as those of us who are deficient in them often feel, in attempting to make up a deliberate opinion upon any book,—that these are absolutely necessary, to enable us to determine what works of the day we may read with profit, or what might tend to pervert our taste, take the bloom off of the freshness of our moral sensibility and belittle our understandings,—and the reversals of cotemporary decisions, which time at length decrees, might teach us all some modesty as to the value of a too hasty judgment,—bringing this one down and setting up another,—and our own experience of the estimate we place, to-day, upon those writings, over whose pages we wept or laughed, a month ago, and which we do not care much to look upon again,—tend very much to show the importance of a higher and sounder standard of criticism, than can be conveniently maintained in the columns of a daily newspaper.

But I do claim, that the lavish and indiscriminate praise bestowed by the newspaper-press, often with a strange unanimity, upon swarm after swarm of worthless and sometimes really pernicious writings, argues either a blindness of judgment, which requires much enlightenment, or a willingness to tamper with the best interests of society, demanding its emphatic reprobation. I do earnestly object and protest against a practice, degrading to the press and treacherous to its trust, under which it sacrifices that impartial expression of opinion, which is the sole test of its independence, and the only basis of its utility, and thus betrays the public confidence, by selling literary judgment, which should be above price, to be valuable at all,—by permitting its sheets to become the mere vehicles of those, whose only object is pecuniary gain,—and by thus dragging folly, impudence and vice through all the fœtid channels of society, and often, over paths of fresher fragrance and purer light, where only innocence and peace ought to enjoy the loving and secure domain. As if it were not enough for the press, in some of its manifestations, to come forward *in forma pauperis*, and make appeals of solicitation to the public sympathy and support, which may not be unreasonable, when they are really deserved,—or, in other moods, to assume a bolder front, and claim for its dictates the sanctity of supreme law,—to insinuate, that he, who does not study their columns, might as well neglect all other studies,—to remind the thoughtless multitude of direful and complicated disasters, always impending over that unwary, and now, I suppose, merely hypothetical individual, *who does not take the papers*,—as if it were not enough, by thus pushing their own circulation, to have substituted, in a great measure, for the solid food of the mind, lucubrations, often excellent, but which, every intelligent editor knows, afford, after all, a very unsatisfactory repast for the hungry mind,—so that the very elements of our mental growth, the guides of our youth, the refreshment of our manhood, the solace of our age, the material of our reflection, and the inspiration of our progress towards the stars,—the secret fountains of good literature, whence the soul draws vigor only upon diligent quest, must be unsought (for who does, or who can find time for this, if his restless thirst for knowledge is momentarily allayed by these trickling way-side rills ?)—as if this were not quite enough to disorder the faculties and to enervate the strength of the general mind,—still more,—in the indulgence of a growing venality, many, certainly not all, must lend themselves to purposes of popular deception, notorious to the well-informed; and if they do not themselves dress up falsehood, yet allow her to be so arrayed at the foot of their own tribunal, and thence issue forth in the stolen habiliments of truth, —making her thus appear sectarian and factious, who ought to be universal,—consenting to the irresponsible creation and announcement of a thousand narrow, partizan, and yet extravagant reputations, truly bubbles,—and selling incalculable mischief for a paltry consideration,—until, at length, in the very nature of the case, a sort of conventional condition of things would be likely to grow up,—so that neither would the editor be expected to mean what he alleged, nor would anybody, but the unsuspicious, be expected so to understand him,—and nothing would be so varnished and insincere as newspaper praise,—nothing so truly fictitious, as a wide-spread literary reputation, when it had been thus gained, and, at length, the general and apparently spontaneous laudation of the press might be almost assumed to be a general conspiracy for public fraud.

Indeed, one would seem, sometimes, almost driven to the conclusion, that newspapers conceive it their business to praise most those books, which undoubtedly need the most charitable consideration of their character; and that the critical opinion expressed, is not so much the result of a fair judgment of the merits, as it is evidence of some morbid sympathy, touched by the very defects of the production. A well-regulated and truthful mind will accord praise only to deserving objects. One which is ill-regulated is little disposed to admit the claims of anything, which is superior to its own capacity; but rather flatters its own self-estimate, perhaps, in bestowing compliments upon whatever it accounts inferior to itself; because, in the latter instance, its native vanity is not necessarily lowered. And sometimes, we may fear, that, in this world of ours, men endeavor to escape the contempt to which they are themselves subject, by striving to debase others to their own level.

Besides, in order to exercise criticism justly, judgment, taste and skill, as well as a mind open to fair impressions, are essential, while none of these qualities are requisite, to enable the writer to pile up elaborate generalizations of praise. The consequence is, that the latter style of remark is often employed, in these vehicles, when the editor knows not what else to say; and, frequently, commendation is so lavished upon unworthy objects, that a just and reasonable expression of approbation, of a really meritorious, useful and valuable work, would seem almost like censure itself, it falls so much below the exaggerated and extravagant criterion of ordinary encomium. For truth and excellence these newspapers, as we would benevolently conclude, often appear to imagine, can take care of themselves,—and so they leave them to the chances of good or ill-fortune; while every veritable imposture really seems to elicit all their good offices; and they assist it to puff and swell itself up into a vain show, and thus to deceive the populace, which of itself is sufficiently resolved on being deceived. And they thus forget or betray the doctrine of a sentiment, as wise and useful now, as when it was first pronounced—*Virtus rectorem, ducemque desiderat, vitia sine magistro discuntur.*

These opinions may seem bold,—but they would require much more firmness for their expression, if the more intelligent and well-disposed of the class indicated were not already sensible of great defects and evils, of this and other descriptions, in the management of newspapers,—and if these ordinary means of public information and enlightenment were not already groaning under many burdens of this sort, which they know not how to lift,—and if I did not feel confident, that all the honest conductors of the press will rejoice in whatever shall do something towards their relief, by directing public attention to a great and growing mischief, in the correction of which the public is so deeply interested.

Is there any remedy for this evil? To the honor of whatever is best in society, be it said, that, although vast mischiefs, already existing, owe their origin and their continuance to the unbridled license, the indiscretion and the ignorance and falsity of a portion of the press,—that, though by their means feverish excitements have been fanned, leading to deadly disorders in the body politic and social,—though from this source the minds of the young have been poisoned, the peace of families has been destroyed, the authority of wisdom, virtue and experience set at naught, the purity of life polluted, and a flippant, mocking, disbelieving spirit sent current into the ordinary avenues of the community—yet the growing indifference to the opinions of newspapers, once carrying weight and authority,—not to be ascertained, perhaps, by the statistics of their circulation, but in the fact, that the public look to them, more and more, as mere matters of amusement and vehicles of ordinary intelligence, —shows that society will demand something more reliable, and suggests to them the necessity of a more judicious management and a more elevated tone. I am not willing, for one, to pay a servile homage to the formal or informal dissertations of a newspaper, written, as I happen to know, by a certain definable individual, perhaps, an acquaintance or friend, whose capacity and standard may be accurately guaged, although he may be supposed to represent, and may misrepresent, the opinions of any sect, or clique, or combination. But I respect his calling,—I value his opportunities of usefulness,—I honor and prize his power to disseminate valuable information, and the vast capacity of his means to promote that true aim of all rational society,—a community of good-feeling, intelligence and virtue. Him I personally esteem more than ordinary men,—his press I hold as a just exemplification of the choicest blessing of human invention,—when he honestly dedicates his abilities to this beneficent purpose, and speeds the winged messengers of thought upon so charitable a mission.

When I consider how fluctuating is public opinion, —how readily popular sentiment may be raised or depressed, by the operation of external influences brought steadily and continuously to bear upon it, and how much the cause of true knowledge and true freedom is dependent upon the current expression of public thought,—I could wish, if it were possible, that some higher standard might be contrived by human ingenuity, for the authorized tone of newspaper speculation. If it be assumed, that the march of human events is to place society eventually in a more elevated position, than it has heretofore attained,—since, obviously, this could be the result only of its intellectual and moral advancement,—that is, of the higher control conquered by our supersensible faculties over our material nature,—it follows, that, unless the means of progress are really of a character calculated to promote, rather than retard an event so desirable, the position is itself erroneous. Taking into view, therefore, the fact of the extraordinary circulation secured by the newspaper press,—and that, by its demands upon our time, and by means of its creation and encouragement of a popular taste, it has contrived to substitute itself, in a great measure, for former sources of mental refreshment and discipline,—the writings of poets, orators, philosophers and historians,—whose speculations are concerned about the essential elements of life, and whose works are approved by the deliberate judgment of mankind,—it becomes us to inquire, if this new instrument of progress be in advance, or behind,—above or below, the actual necessities of the times. Are those, who, by the force of circumstances, have gained this extraordinary facility of intercourse with the masses of the community, entitled to their preëminent advantages of influence, upon their merits and their honor,—adding living stones, day by day, to the growing structure, which is eventually to constitute the perfect and completed edifice of human good? Or, are they pursuing,—as neither poets, orators, philosophers or historians, who have acquired any permanent fame, have ever done,—a temporizing policy, likely to accelerate the downward impulse of general deterioration?

If we rely upon newspapers, instead of thinking for ourselves, we have really constituted a numerous body of public instructors, leading public sentiment, moulding public morals, forming public and private character, effecting great changes in our social condition, working to some end, and, therefore, undermining, if they are not strengthening, the foundations of our civil rights; and it is high time public attention were awakened to the fact. But why should not those, who are to educate the people, be themselves educated, for the public service, upon the public responsibility? For education, by which is meant the complete training of the mind, and, if you please, the body,—though it renders no man perfect,—does tend to the enlargement of his faculties and the elevation of his soul,—so that they, who come from the select company of those, who, in all ages, have dignified and glorified the condition of manhood, are less susceptible of mean views,—less liable to petty temptations,—less easily controlled and led away, by the madness of the populace demanding infamous compliances. I am sure, I should be glad to see a college, or a commission established, to settle upon a firmer and fairer basis the theory of editorial qualifications,—not certainly rendering such training indispensable, because this might be to erect a censorship, dangerously interfering with the just exercise of popular liberty,—but to raise the standard of instruction, in ethics, as well as in learning, amongst those, whose duty and whose privilege it is to teach. I know not why, in this way, the whole corps editorial, like the learned professions, in this and all other civilized countries, might not eventually and safely be placed, under the guidance and protection of the law. Is such an idea impracticable or inexpedient? Or, is it not rather an object of the clearest common concern, that the requirements of this profession should be such, as to warrant its pretensions to be ranked amongst the highest intellectual pursuits, and so to make its influence as beneficial, as it is already widely extensive? We establish schools, under the law, and with suitable regulations, for the purpose of converting boys and girls into such men and women, as shall adorn and bless society,—and I see not how this great public school of morals and of knowledge should fail of converting men and women into children again, unless a correcter public sentiment should regulate its license, and give the spur to a more honorable ambition.

I sincerely trust, that none of those, whom I have had the honor to address, this evening, will have misapprehended the true scope of my views, or the just nature of my motives. I know not how any abuse can stand a chance of reformation, unless it be fairly and freely presented to the public ordeal, and brought to the test of that judgment, often momentarily erroneous, seldom wilfully and permanently perverse. I have not discharged a duty, which many might consider thankless and even invidious,—so much are we the slaves of opinion,—because I look upon the Press, taking its abuses, together with what it has of enlightened and legitimate action, as anything else, than the most available and indispensable common instrument of human progress,—but because I would see it shake off some of its modern vices, and reïnstate itself in public confidence, and grow with it to a nobler stature, by a juster and more generous administration of its powers. My only fear is, that I have been unable to do the work proposed, even if it were in my power at all, so thoroughly as I had hoped, within the limited compass of a single lecture. I have expressed these opinions, because I entertain them. I do not know, that any one has undertaken formally to present the subject in this light before. I have consulted no authority and have read no book. My views, such as they are, are the result of some experience and means of observation, and of a great deal of inevitable reflection. I seek only for the press, that it may be entitled to a higher honor, and enjoy a wider sphere of usefulness. I would have it, therefore, manly, vigorous, thoughtful, generous, elevated, just and sincere. Upon this mature development of its character will very much depend its future influence upon popular sentiment; and it is the manifestation of this sentiment, which is to advance or retard the substantial improvement of mankind.

NOTE.—While this volume is going to press, the author makes the following extract from a leading New York paper, the application of which to his whole subject is obvious. "Party-spirit pervades nearly the whole press,—religious as well as secular; and every paper, in the interest of any party, whether moral, ecclesiastical or political, resorts to devices for promoting its ends, which a rigid judgment would probably be compelled to regard as immoral."

MR. MACAULAY

ON

WARREN HASTINGS.

It is now more than forty years ago, since two young Americans, who at that period happened to be in London, amongst other objects of curiosity and interest, were induced to visit Lansdowne-House, then the town-residence of the Marquis of Lansdowne, well-known, in his day, in the circles of politics and letters. It is understood, that the show-palaces of the English nobility are to be seen by strangers, only in the absence of their proprietors; and, in the present instance, the owner had been some time absent, at some one of his residences in the country. Accordingly, the Americans were introduced into the house; and, in the course of their perambulation of the premises and inspection of library and paintings, were conducted to an apartment, containing only two pictures. One of these every American would at once recognize, as the unmistakable portrait of the Father of his Country; the other proved to be the counterfeit presentment of a personage, then scarcely less known to fame; and was, in fact, the portrait of Warren Hastings, for many years, the Governor-general of India. It so happened, however, that, during their visit, Lord Lansdowne unexpectedly returned to town, and, understanding that there were strangers examining the house, courteously proceeded to the room, where our young friends were engaged; and entering into conversation with them, informed them, that he appropriated this privileged apartment to these two pictures alone, as being the portraits of the two greatest men he had ever known.

The Americans said nothing; and, as that was not the age of "free discussion," felt, perhaps, that it might be uncivil to call in question even the most eccentric fancies of a gentleman, in his own house. But the saying sank deep into their memory; and when one of the parties, some time since, gave me the particulars of the adventure, it struck my mind, I must confess, as a thing of peculiar incongruity. Washington and Warren Hastings! The savior of his country—and the desolator of an oppressed and ruined people! This one, the living spirit of all that is known as truth, wisdom, honor, moderation and integrity in man,—that one, the cruel and unjust tool of a grasping and insatiable avarice! This man, at the close of all his patient and heroic toils, in the great struggle, to which his own prudence and brave policy, by the blessing of Heaven, had brought success,—claiming no reward of his country, and accepting only the bare repayment of so much, as he had expended, from his own fortune, in her service; the other, rioting upon extorted bribes, and returning from the land, which his injustice had made wretched, to receive, in charity, at last, the means of sustaining his prolonged existence, from the coffers which had been so often replenished by his own wickedness! The one, retiring from the cares of public life, amidst the grateful tears of a reluctant people, followed by the admiration of the world and secure of the benedictions of posterity; the other, disgracefully recalled from the distant world, where his crimes had made the name of Englishman a scourge and a dread; met, upon his native shore, by the execrations of the populace and the stern rebuke of the highest, the brightest and the purest spirits of his country's glorious days; impeached by the Commons of England, in the name of the people whom he had wronged, and for the sake of the humanity which he had outraged; and after a trial, enduring for a longer series of years than that, within which his compatriot of Lansdowne-House had achieved the liberties of the republic,—finally escaping, amidst the tergiversations of political factions, the wearisomeness of protracted justice, and the influence of a spirit, which submitted to prefer interest to honor—and could not well preserve its consistency by condemning the culprit, after it had accepted and appropriated his bribe.

The anecdote, which I have just detailed, was brought forcibly to my recollection, in reading, some time since, the brilliant and seductive article of Mr. Macaulay, upon the character and administration of Hastings. The subject, considered in its connections, is one of vast importance, inasmuch as it relates to the commencement and extension of British power in Asia, and the influence of this domination upon the interests, the morals and the happiness of the world. But the Essay of Mr. Macaulay, with all its elaborate splendor of diction and graphic profusion of illustration, did not satisfy my judgment, for precisely the same reason, that the juxtaposition of the portraits of Washington and Hastings did not coincide with the preconceptions of the young Americans at Lansdowne-House. To estimate the character of an individual, by setting his vices in parallel with his abilities and their unscrupulous exercise for the acquisition of dominion and riches, for himself or others, may indeed tend to dazzle and bewilder the imagination. But when we come to compare such a man with him, who has devoted his powers to the unquestionable benefit of his race, or, which is better, to try him by the unerring standard of truth and justice itself, the fallacy becomes apparent to the most cursory apprehension. It cannot be denied, that the world is not too apt to make the necessary and reasonable distinction between the uses of great ability, accordingly as it is well or ill employed; or to remember that the sole legitimate purpose, as well as the only merit of knowledge, consists in the enlargement of virtue; and if we could but escape subjection to that inverse rule of morals, by which the world calls "good evil and evil good," we might demand, that the highest intellect should be but the measure and standard of the most consummate goodness. In the Court of Heaven, we know that the perversion of talents is to be regarded criminal, in proportion to their amount and superiority. At the tribunal of worldly judgment, the very possession of distinguished powers is too often looked upon as a sufficient palliation for their abuse.

I shall not allege, that the Essay of Mr. Macaulay is in any sense a panegyric. He professes, indeed, to assume the attitude of an impartial judge. He neither imitates the miserable adulation of Mr. Gleig, whose Biography of Hastings he reviews; nor is he stirred up to the just severity, honestly exhibited by Mill, in his History of British India. He pretends to deprecate, on the one hand, any deference to that caprice of popular favor, which induced the House of Commons in 1813, to rise up in honor of a man, who, twenty-seven years before, had escaped the punishment of his crimes, through the technicalities of the law; and, on the other, Mr. Burke's spirit of indignant denunciation, which compelled Hastings himself to acknowledge, at the close of one of those terrible philippics, that he "felt himself to be the most guilty man alive,"—"until," he continued, "he appealed to his conscience and was reassured." But besides the advancement of occasional theories in morals, adapted, it is to be feared, rather to the vitiated taste of the times, than to the requirements of the eternal rule of right, there is a dazzling series of picturesque descriptions, and a display of gorgeous scenery, more like the allurements of romance, than homely and natural truth, and all so clothed in a veil of enchanting language, that it is difficult to separate the character of the freebooter from his successes and to remember, as we are led to the conclusion, that it is, after all, like dragging a criminal, in a triumphal car to the place of his execution, and crowning with fruitless laurels the head, which, the next moment, is to find its brotherhood with the clod.

And this, in truth, is the chief subject of complaint against Mr. Macaulay. Not, that he does not rebuke with sufficient severity some of those instances of the conduct of Hastings, which, indeed, could admit of no defence; nor, that he leaves entirely out of his account many of the more flagrant examples of cruel and rapacious injustice, which signalized his administration; but that he covers up truth with sophistical extenuation; that he palliates infamy by the enforcements of expediency; that he admits his hero to have resolved deliberately upon the accomplishment of evil purposes, and then urges the necessity of evil means, in order to secure success; that, while he leads the careful reader almost to apprehend some deficiency in the moral perceptions of the brilliant essayist, he leaves the less discriminating, at least in doubt, whether Hastings, though unquestionably guilty of grave offences, was not, on the whole, a persecuted and injured man; that he seems to justify a conclusion, that the world has wasted much declamation, for some thousands of years, against mercenary and ambitious conquest; and bewilders us onwards to the treacherous inference, that even he may be deserving of admiration, if not respect, whose only claim to merit, upon his own showing, consisted in extending British dominion over a country, to which she had not the shadow of a right, and in transmitting to his employers immense treasures, obtained constantly by means, for which even Hastings himself does not pretend to set up any defence.

It is no part of my purpose, to enter upon any detailed account of this remarkable man. A dreaming and romantic boy, at his native village of Daylesford, there mingled with his earliest reflections the resolution to recover those paternal possessions, with which his impoverished ancestors had been compelled to part; and this idea, which he never lost sight of, until its final realization, together with the hope of reviving an extinguished family title, afford a plausible key to much of his subsequent career. At a very early age he was admitted to the civil service of the East India Company. By the exertion of his extraordinary endowments and the fortunate concurrence of events, he was soon raised to a post of great trust and emolument. One of the earliest incidents in his political life, not even alluded to by Mr. Macaulay, was his intervention, as interpreter, in an infamous plot, contrived between some of the English agents and certain native functionaries, for the deposition of one prince and the assassination of another. As all the revolutions, which were brought about in India, were promoted for the acquisition of money,—besides the incidental benefit to the parties concerned, the Company eventually realized between £200,000 and £300,000 by this creditable transaction. When, some time afterwards, a report of its character was brought to the knowledge of the Directors in London, they transmitted orders to the Council for its investigation. This board consisted of three individuals, of whom Hastings was one. His connection with the business seemed to disqualify him for the position of a judge. In order to remove this impediment, Mr. Hastings prepared a statement, in which he alleged, that he did not recollect acting as interpreter, and that he thought he should remember it, if he had, in fact, been present in that capacity. Nor can we, on our part, doubt, that he must easily have recalled the particulars of transactions so important, occurring within the previous two or three years. To corroborate the account given by Hastings, another of the accomplices, who, while the transaction was fresh, had made affidavit that Hastings did so act, now recalled his former statement, and affirmed that he conceived he must have been mistaken, in his original deposition, and believed, that *he himself* was in reality the interpreter on the occasion in question. The Council, thus conveniently composed, constituted the tribunal, which was to judge of the weight of the precious testimony submitted for the mutual exculpation. In fact, the recollections of the whole party became finally extremely indistinct, and they thus proceeded, with clear judgment, to the honorable acquittal of all persons concerned!

The period elapsing, between the retirement of Clive and the accession of Hastings to the Presidency of Bengal, exhibited that country in an aspect, which had never before been witnessed, on such a scale, in the history of the world. There was literally nothing like civil government throughout its territories. The native Prince, who still retained his title and every show of outward respect, possessed not even the slightest shadow of authority. The English power, which, commencing with the establishment of an insignificant trading-fort and factory, at Calcutta, had seized, on what might, perhaps, be considered some reasonable pretext, to secure the mastery of the province, still submitted to the style of 'vassals of the throne of Delhi;' and the Council, which represented the Company at home, employed its energies almost entirely upon negotiations for the benefit and furtherance of trade. With no constitution, therefore, or form of civil government, or system of recognized law; indeed, without any responsible political head, since the supreme authority, which existed at the council-board, was altogether devoted to the requirements of mercantile affairs, rather than to the administration of justice, it is not strange that unheard-of abuses and excesses ravaged and desolated the land. The natives dared not resist the most unwarrantable assumptions. Every Englishman, in fact, did not what was right, but what seemed most profitable in his own eyes. Trade, instead of a just and honorable commerce, for the mutual benefit, became a system of thorough and unscrupulous pillage. And, as no foreigner resided in India, except for the purpose of amassing a fortune, the infamous rapidity, with which this object could be effected, rather than any consideration of the just means, was the ruling principle of all classes of Europeans, throughout this unhappy land. It is matter of eternal and indelible disgrace to the English name, that, for a series of fifteen years, from 1756, the commencement of British domination in Asia, to the accession of Hastings, in 1771, such remained the true condition of this wretched and distracted country. The issue of that revolution, which had secured the rights of conquest to an enlightened and Christian nation, imposed upon it equally the duties of moral government and the establishment of civil polity. And if the very peculiarities of this singular people, and those deep-rooted prejudices, which, deducing their origin in some remote period of undiscovered antiquity, had preserved their personal habits and their social organization the same, under every influx of foreign invasion and through successive internal revolutions, in spite of Mussulman bigotry and the intermixture of a hundred races, in defiance alike of the Mahometan sword and the more peaceful weapons of the Christian church militant; if these things rendered them less likely to be readily influenced even by the highest exemplification of principles, which our religion professes as its plainest duties, —one thing is certain, they had become dependent on their invaders, and were entitled to protection in the common rights, and to security for the ordinary privileges of humanity. Almost all conquerors, in every stage of society, appear to have had some compunctions upon this subject. They have established law, at least for the maintenance of their own authority, if not for the direct benefit of those whom they have subdued. The very Tamerlane himself, who, three hundred and fifty years before, had founded on conquest in India that great Mogul Empire, the legal dominion of which the English in Bengal acknowledged, at least, in name,—had endeavored, in some measure, to cultivate, in peace, those principles of public and private conduct, without which peace itself never can be desirable. And of the volume, called the "Institutions of Tamerlane," which he left, as a sacred legacy to his posterity, Mr. Burke declares, that he believes "there is not a book in the world, which contains nobler, more just, more manly, more pious principles of government." Abused and perverted it had undoubtedly been; but unfortunately we need not travel so far, as to India within the Ganges, for examples of violated constitutions and outraged laws. At all events, the English were bound to provide their subjects, with a system as salutary, as that which they had broken in pieces. And if they had indeed done so, the announcement of Christian doctrine might have been much more efficacious, than after every prejudice had been enlisted, every hostile feeling engendered, and the manners of the people had become tenfold more corrupted, under every experience of plunder and cruel and lawless violence.

It was at this period of disorder and insecurity, that so many of those enormous fortunes were amassed, which made a proverb of the titles, as well as transferred the wealth of the native princes, to the crowds of Englishmen in India; that so many *nabobs*, so called, returned home, with consciences oftentimes as shattered as their constitutions, to linger out their days, amidst those spoils of extortion, which they had no longer the power to enjoy; and those magnificent dreams of oriental riches were indeed realized, which overloaded a few, at the expense of miserable millions of mankind. It was in the course of these and a few succeeding years, that the immense amount of two hundred millions of dollars was transported from the one country to the other; and that England, before this time, if not a poor, yet far from being a wealthy country, but maintaining its respectability with its old honest independence, and for the most part homely and virtuous, became dazzled with this sudden influx of riches and its easy means of acquisition; yielded to the corrupt influence of a general profusion, to which its people had not been accustomed; and, losing much principle and self-respect, in the countenance not withheld, if not cordially extended to the returning nabobs, the public mind became at length, more or less vitiated; nor is it matter of vain speculation, to infer, that the nation is, at this day, struggling in consequence, under many of the just and unavoidable evils, which result from ill-gotten wealth.

But if such was the condition of India, at the time of the elevation of Hastings to the Presidency of Bengal, certainly never was a fairer field displayed, for the exercise of his splendid abilities, if they had been directed and controlled by the nobler qualities of human nature. A wise and just administration of his government was demanded of him, no less by what was due to the character of England, than by the sufferings of the people of Hindostan. The cries, which so long had appealed to the mercies of the ever-opening heavens; the evils, which seem sometimes to be permitted, in order to test our use or abuse of the faculties with which we are endowed,—had, at length, extorted counsels and orders from the Directors, for the reformation of what was indeed a scene of almost unmitigated horrors. Instead of this, his administration was but one long conflict with the better spirit of his colleagues in the government; one continued act of disobedience to the directions, if not to the wishes of his employers at home.

Mr. Macaulay crowns his final encomium of the career of Hastings, with the assertion that he "founded a polity." It would be a more just judgment, to aver, that he extended a usurpation. The same conduct of affairs, which would have exposed a private citizen to the general execration of mankind, exhibited here on an enlarged scale, carried forward with unscrupulous boldness and terminating in complete success,—if it has not secured Hastings from the obloquy of history, has given his name a distinguished place, upon that doubtful file, at which many well-disposed persons are willing to look, with a certain indefinite feeling of wonder and admiration. According to the principles of worldly judgment, in its most worldly sense, Hastings no doubt acted wisely, in the course, which he determined to pursue. He knew well, that men do not, as a general rule, more strictly enquire into the moral character of an agent, who never fails to furnish them with all that they demand, than Aladdin, in the Arabian Nights, thought of questioning the legal authority of the Genius of the Lamp; and he conceived that he could make no reply so satisfactory, to the reiterated complaints from home, on the subject of his injustice and extortion, as the liberal remittance of unquestionable *lacs of rupees.* Like the Irish absentee landlord, who commands his factor not to rack-rent his tenants, but yet insists on his immediate occasion for a thousand pounds,—the Board of Directors filled their letters to the Governor-general, with various weighty resolutions of disapprobation, and issued voluminous homilies, full of the most virtuous and exemplary remonstrance; but never failed to insinuate, that the necessities of the Company imperatively demanded a fresh supply of the one indispensable commodity!

Mr. Macaulay conceives Hastings to have been thus placed in a situation of great difficulty. In the embarrassed condition of the country which he governed, he had no present means of raising money, except by robbery, and the argument is, that it was, therefore, necessary for him to turn buccaneer. But his position, in fact, required him to make his election, between his true duty to the trusts reposed in him, on both sides of the great ocean, which separated the dependant from his masters, controlled by his duty to himself, and to a higher Power, of whom he seems never to have thought,—and the commission of great crimes. "He had no choice left him," observes Mr. Macaulay, "except to commit great wrongs, or to resign all his hopes of fortune and distinction." To a really honest mind there would, of course, be no difficulty in making the election. To a mind, constituted like that of Hastings, there was equally no difficulty, for he evidently never entertained a scruple upon the subject. His principle of action is well laid down by Mr. Macaulay himself. "He seems to have held it a fundamental proposition, which could not be disputed, that when he had not as many lacs of rupees as the public service required, he was to take them from any body who had." And again—"The rules of justice, the sentiments of humanity, the plighted faith of treaties, were in his view as nothing, when opposed to the immediate interests of the state." But even allowing that the requirements of public necessity excuse, if they do not justify much occasional wrong, the heartless depravity of such principles and practices does not admit of the extenuation thus sophistically suggested; for here was no "public service," except that created to gratify the grasping avarice of Hastings and his employers, and the necessities of the Company itself constituted the only "interests of the state." And it would be, indeed, difficult, to recall many distinguished personages, out of Bulwer's novels, who quite come up to the deformity of character, thus incidentally developed! Cortez we might instance, perhaps, with some more show of apology; Pizarro, it would be safe to judge a better man, for though he too robbed and murdered, yet he regarded the heathenish Peruvians, much as the prophet of old looked upon Agag and the company of Amalek; and if he destroyed cities to-day, he founded and built up others to-morrow.

The passages I have quoted will serve to justify Mr. Macaulay, in an occasional moral reflection upon what he gently styles the "faults" of the Governor-general, almost concealed, as they are, in the flowery emblazonment of his career, and neutralized by the implied approbation of his eventful life. But in a government, conducted upon motives like those set forth, the excesses and barbarities, by which it was distinguished, would follow as the necessary and unavoidable consequence. It is not strange that these things roused the eventual indignation of English society, which is something, by the way, never to be confounded, in that country, more than in our own, with the policy of the government, or the acts of public bodies; nor is it singular, that eventually the offender should have been called to answer for his crimes, while there was anything resembling the common attributes of morality, justice or religion remaining in the world.

I am willing to make every reasonable allowance for the peculiar attitude and relations of the public accusers of Hastings and their principal leader, Mr. Burke; and however differences may exist, as to some of Mr. Burke's political speculations, in the estimation of friend and foe alike, few men have ever lived of more unblemished purity of purpose and more perfect integrity of mind and heart. His language upon opening the charges against Hastings is exceedingly strong. "The crimes," he says upon the occasion alluded to, "which we charge in these articles are not lapses, defects, errors of common human frailty, which, as we know and feel, we can allow for. We charge this offender with no crimes, that have not arisen from passions, which it is criminal to harbor; with no offences, that have not their root in avarice, rapacity, pride, insolence, ferocity, treachery, cruelty, malignity of temper; in short, in nothing that does not argue a total extinction of all moral principle; that does not manifest an inveterate blackness of heart, dyed in grain with malice, vitiated, corrupted, gangrened to the very core. If we do not plant his crimes in those vices, which the breast of man is made to abhor, and the spirit of all laws, human and divine, to interdict, we desire no longer to be heard on this occasion. * * * We urge no crimes that were not crimes of forethought. We charge him with nothing, that he did not commit upon deliberation; that he did not commit against advice, supplication and remonstrance; that he did not commit against the direct command of lawful authority; that he did not commit after reproof and reprimand; the reproof and reprimand of those, who are authorized by the laws to reprove and reprimand him. * * * He was fourteen years at the head of that service, and there is not an instance, no, not one single instance, in which he endeavored to detect corruption, or that he ever, in any one single instance, attempted to punish it; but the whole service, with that whole mass of enormity which he attributes to it, slept as it were at once under his terror and his protection; under his protection, if they did not dare to move against him; under his terror, from his power to pluck out individuals and make a public example of them, whenever he saw fit. And therefore, that service, under his guidance and influence, was even beyond what its own nature disposed it to, a service of confederacy, a service of connivance, a service composed of various systems of guilt, of which Mr. Hastings was the head and protector."

It is not often that the most austere and ferocious tyrant is more forcibly portrayed. And if we can indeed conceive of a man totally deficient in the common sentiments of justice and humanity, or totally averse to their application, we may form some judgment of the probable course and current of events, likely to distinguish his administration. It is scarcely possible, without entering more minutely into the subject than I intend, even to allude intelligibly to intricate affairs like these, often dependent, for their full understanding, upon various circumstantial details and explanations. It would be in vain to emulate the highly-wrought illustrations of the Essay of Mr. Macaulay. But I shall endeavor to present what I have thought it important to consider, with all reasonable clearness to your good sense and judgment.

I have already remarked, that Hastings found the finances of Bengal in a state of considerable embarrassment. In order to meet this exigency, he did not attempt to stem the current of abuses, nor, as is the fashion of modern legislators, to call into play the invaluable services of an able and judicious committee of retrenchment. But wisely reflecting that, since all Englishmen in India were there, for the purpose of making money, by fair means or foul, it would be a pity to disturb them in so laudable a pursuit, he left them altogether to their own devices, and looked about him, on his part, for native princes of reputed riches, to insult, and upon any show of displeasure, to plunder without mercy or compunction. In fact, nothing could be more simple and efficacious, than the process by which Hastings raised the necessary remittances. It must be remembered, that, in the earlier part of his administration, he was only the governor of Bengal, which province was held by the East India Company solely for the purposes of commerce. The Empire of Hindostan, of which Bengal made a portion, consisted of a great number of principalities, more or less independent, although nominally owning subjection to the descendant of Tamerlane at Delhi. The Empire had become thoroughly disorganized, after the successful invasion of the great Persian conqueror, Nadir Shah, in the early part of the eighteenth century. The various viceroys or princes were generally at dissension amongst themselves; and many of them were ambitious of extending their territories and power. Some of these dignitaries had accumulated vast treasures, which Hastings wanted; he, on the other hand, had troops at his command, against whose discipline the bravest native forces were utterly unable to contend. Nothing could be more obvious, therefore, than the course of conduct to be pursued. Whenever the directors at home suggested the propriety of further remittances, Hastings, at once, proceeded to take possession of a province. It sometimes happened, that he was able to effect an amicable arrangement with some one of the superior officers of the reigning prince, and rewarded his treachery by installing him in the place of his deposed master, at a stipulated and always an extremely remunerative price. In case an arrangement of this kind could not be conveniently made, he disposed of the stolen province, by sale, to the nearest potentate, who was willing to become the purchaser. By means like these, he was able, in less than two years, to add something like £700,000 to the annual revenue of "The Honorable, the Company of Merchants, trading to the East Indies," besides sending home about £1,000,000, in ready money.

The sad and painful history of the unfortunate Princesses of Oude, the two aged and noble women, out of whose protracted sufferings he at length wrung £1,200,000, by a course of absolutely unparalleled barbarities,—at least since the days of Montezuma and Guatemozin,—not only without pretence, but against every emotion which human nature loves,—

has long prompted the indignant horror of those, who are acquainted with the history of the concluding years of the last century. It is difficult to imagine, how a mind, actuated by much reverence for the principles of common honesty, can entertain any different sentiment in regard to other similar instances of atrocity and oppression ; such as the Rohilla war, the execution of the Brahmin Nuncomar, the sack of Dinagepore, the infamous exactions at Benares, and innumerable other acts of treachery and violence, some of which are alluded to, while others do not seem even to have attracted the attention of Mr. Macaulay. It would make the heart too sick, to undertake the recital, or to endure the relation of things, which, in their enormity and extent, surpass all that history or fable have recorded, at least amongst the fruits of peace, if they are not equally eminent above all the more ordinary ferocities of war. And the lapse of more than seventy years, and the gradual influence of a generally more humane and improving legislation, have not been able to efface them from the memory of the people of India. If it were possible to conceive of an anomaly so strange and unheard of, as a demon of peace itself,—only not the genius of War, because all the power, all the cruelty and all the desire to prey upon the defenceless, were rioting at its single heart,—some idea may be formed of the condition of this unhappy land, under the terrible visitation of its destroyer. Hastings himself and many after him have set up the plea, that the people of Hindostan were but a nation, whom nature and habit had fitted only for slaves; and that they would endure no treatment but that, to which a treacherous slave should be subjected by a rigorous master. But, without staying to inquire into the duties, which we may conclude to devolve upon the humane and Christian superior, to whom Providence intrusts the welfare of the dependant,—the plea itself is untenable, for the reason that it is not true. That the standard of general morals was not higher in Hindostan, than in many other semi-barbarous countries, we may well believe. That this standard had become depreciated, in proportion as you approached the sea-coast, where foreigners chiefly congregated, we have also some reason for believing to be quite credible. The natives had been, for a long time, subjected to the evils of anarchy, and they had not gained any improvement by their intercourse with Europeans. There are certain offences which a Hindoo never forgives, chiefly relating to his caste and his personal dignity; as is the case, in the latter particular, at least, with every unchristianized people. If they have strong faults of character, they are no less distinguished by many kinds of virtue, which it were to be wished were more common and more valued in Europe and America. No doubt, they are acute, intelligent and crafty. In the encounter of wits, the English often had to submit to be foiled in their own game of plunder. Resenting such successes, as injuries, therefore, they looked with suspicion upon all those more prominent Indian qualities; and they were especially provoked at any reluctance (unpardonable in slaves), to aid their generous design of transferring the gold and the silver, the jewels, the ivory, the silks and the spices,—in truth, the riches of the Indies,—to the "fast-anchored isle of the ocean;" and, for all these reasons, the invaders contrived to fix upon the subjected a very discreditable name.

In order to show, that I do not make allegations without proof, I quote, as to the character of, at least, a portion of the inhabitants of Bengal, a few words from a book, written by a predecessor of Hastings in the Presidency, while the English domination was yet insecure; and it is of the more authority, because the object of the author was to persuade to a compliance with his scheme, for the subversion of the Hindu government.

"In truth," says this author, Mr. Holwell, "it would be almost cruelty to molest this happy people; for in this district are the only vestiges of the beauty, purity, piety, regularity, equity and strictness of the ancient Hindostan government. Here, the property, as well as the liberty of the people are inviolate. Here, no robberies are heard of, either public or private. The traveller, either with or without merchandise, becomes the immediate care of the government, which allots him guards, without any expense, to conduct him from stage to stage; and these are accountable for the safety of his person and effects. At the end of the first stage, he is delivered over, with certain benevolent formalities, to the guards of the next, who, after interrogating him, as to the usage he has received, in his journey, dismiss the first guard with a written certificate of their behavior, and a receipt for the traveller and his effects; which certificate and receipt are returnable to the commanding officer of the first stage, who registers the same and regularly reports it to the Rajah. In this way, the traveller is passed through the country." And there is much more of the same tenor.

Such also, according to the very highest authority, was the real condition of the people and government of Benares; which city was made by Hastings a scene of injustice and extortion, so utterly indefensible, that Mr. Pitt himself, during the progress of the impeachment,—even after the administration of which he was leader had determined to sustain Hastings,—voted with the opposition as to part of the charges, declaring to Mr. Wilberforce, that his conscience would not let him hold out any longer. In the insecure state of the governments of India, the Rajah of this city and its dependencies paid a fixed tribute to the English authorities for their protection. It is admitted, on all hands, that the tribute was strictly and honorably paid; but the protection proved to be, in the end, such as lambs receive from wolves. The character of this great and magnificent city was somewhat peculiar. It was regarded with religious reverence, throughout all Hindostan. It was filled with schools and colleges and temples of worship. It was constantly crowded with millions of those, who, in that necessity of our nature, which induces certain manifestations of the human mind, in all countries, to aspire to a higher than ordinary tone of religious sentiment, professed, on their part, an uncommon sanctity of character and deportment; and thither the devout Hindoo retired to die. It was what Mecca is to the Mahometan; and what Jerusalem was, to the Hebrew and Christian alike, during a more exalted if not a purer state of religious influence on society. The administration of the Prince had been mild; he was universally beloved and respected; his territory was happy and prosperous. It is said, that nothing could be more striking, than the contrast it presented to the provinces, under the more immediate control of the English government. The tax, paid by the Rajah to the Governor-general, amounted to £50,000 a year, and all he requested in return was, that he and his subjects might be permitted to live in the enjoyment of their own peace and quiet, unmolested by the blessings or the curses of English domination. But the Rajah was reputed to be rich, and the temptation was altogether too strong for the unprincipled cupidity of Hastings. Although the precise total of his subsidy was fixed by solemn engagement, the Rajah submitted, with the best grace he could summon, to repeated additional exactions, until patience could endure it no longer. At length, well knowing the character of his extortioner, and in the hope of buying a permanent peace, he offered Hastings a bribe of £20,000, which the Governor-general accepted, and concealed, and then renewed his demands. Of the event of his unavailing negotiations, his fruitless efforts to avoid an open rupture, and the result of the unhappy Rajah's desperate but vain resistance, it is impossible to speak in terms of sufficient indignation. The Hindoos, in general, are not warlike, and it may be supposed that the minds of a great proportion of the population, commorant in this city of religion, were bent upon peaceful contemplations. Still the people rallied in defence of the sovereign whom they loved and their own liberties; but English arms and terror were at length triumphant. The wretched Prince was compelled to flee forever from his hereditary dominions. Benares was reduced to complete subjection to the invaders. The new Rajah, appointed by the Governor-general, was a mere pensioner upon the English bounty, and (the old consequence) £200,000, annual income, were added to the regular revenues of the Company. The bribe, Hastings, after some time, paid over to the funds of the government. The transaction had, of course, become notorious, and, since it was impossible longer to conceal, it was equally impossible to retain it. The only account he ever gave of the matter was, that he always intended to give the Company credit for it, (although we may remark, they had no more title to it than himself) and, that he, no doubt, had reasons, at the time, for the concealment of its acceptance, but what those reasons were he had entirely forgotten! Nor did he ever inform the public, that he had recalled them to his recollection.

Some years before these occurrences, an event had taken place, which Mr. Burke, in the proceedings of impeachment, did not scruple to brand with the name of murder; and for which, whether viewed in its legal or its moral aspect, it seems difficult to discover a softer name. A specification of charges had been filed at the Council-board, accusing Hastings, amongst other corrupt practices, of taking bribes, on various occasions and to large amounts, for the sale of offices mentioned in the statement. The paper was accompanied by documentary evidence in proof; the sources of oral testimony were pointed out, and the accuser demanded to be personally heard before the Council, in support of his allegations. Nothing could seem a fairer or more open procedure than this. It has been averred by one certainly not friendly to Hastings, yet always considered most friendly to the truth, that there was not an office of justice, or other description, in India, which he did not sell for his own benefit; and the records of the Council would seem fully to sustain this assertion, in the judgment of his colleagues. In their records, not only every matter of public business, but every expression of debate and opinion, were regularly entered, for the inspection of the directors at home. Two of his colleagues were certainly men of the very highest and most unsuspected character; and therefore, we may conclude, justly opposed to the course of his proceedings; nor do I know anything unfavorable to the private reputation of the other member, Sir Philip Francis, except that he appears to have been violent and vindictive in his temper and general demeanor. At all events, they were all equally and openly hostile to the purposes of Hastings. This is one minute, entered at the open Council-board, by General Sir John Clavering:—"In the late proceedings it will appear, that there is no species of peculation, from which the Honorable Governor-general has thought it reasonable to abstain;" and he further adds, in answer to a statement made by Hastings:—"This is only worthy of a man, who has disgraced himself in the eyes of every man of honor both in Asia and Europe."

The Council, as might be concluded, were disposed to proceed in the investigation of the charges preferred against him; but to this Hastings utterly objected, alleging the want of jurisdiction of the tribunal, and the baseness of the accuser himself. The character of this person Mr. Macaulay takes pains to display in the most unfavorable, and, we may believe, the most exaggerated aspect. He alleges all Hindoos to be base, and this person to have been the basest of his race. At all events, if truly described by Hastings and Mr. Macaulay, one would think the head of the government need have had little fear from such a source. The people of India, it is well known, are divided into many hereditary castes. At the head of the very highest and most sacred stood this person, the Brahmin Nuncomar; a Hindoo of the Hindoos; the high priest of a priesthood, claiming peculiar veneration for its order, besides his princely rank amongst the nobility of India. He was possessed of great wealth and immense influence, and the most extraordinary and commanding talents. He was artful, bold, intriguing and perhaps unprincipled. At some of the courts of Europe, he might have passed for a distinguished statesman and patriot, and even from India he exerted no mean influence upon the deliberations of the court of directors in London. So far as I have been able to ascertain, he was elevated by many higher qualities, debased by no meaner vices, than are displayed in the characters of Harley, Sunderland, Bute, Walpole, and other familiar names. It is certain, that he was a politician, eminent for one honorable and generous quality, an earnest of others, the most untiring fidelity to the person and interests of a master, whom Hastings had oppressed and ruined. That he was personally hostile to Hastings, therefore, there can be no doubt, as well on this, as on many other accounts. They had violently quarrelled, some years before ; and the Governor-general hated him besides, because he did not scruple to engage in thwarting many of his unwarrantable designs.

The Council persisted in their investigation of the business, and finally adjudged the charges to be fully sustained. In the meantime, Hastings was unquestionably in great danger, and he resolved upon a step so bold, that, like acts of boldness, oftentimes, it seems to have too much astounded others, both then and since, to permit of their forming an accurate judgment. By his confessed instigation, a charge of forgery, alleged to have been committed six years before, was got up against Nuncomar, upon which he was arrested and thrown into the common jail. In order to bring this question to a successful result, the consent of one other person was requisite. This was Sir Elijah Impey, the chief justice of the Supreme Court of Bengal; a man so execrable, that he has never yet found a defender, for any part of his administration. He had been the school-fellow, and was now the friend of Hastings. To show at once their relations and the moral sense of both, it is only necessary to state, that, although Impey's salary was fixed by law at eight thousand pounds,—upon some difficulty occurring between them, Hastings had secured his connivance, by illegally doubling the amount, from funds within his own control. This was certainly a very convenient arrangement to effect with the judicial check imposed upon his own acts; and the fact proved, that the Governor-general ever after found in Impey a most ready and serviceable instrument. It is said there is no difficulty in procuring testimony of any description in India. However that may be, before this upright judge, with or without evidence, Nuncomar was tried, convicted and sentenced to death; and, to the horror and consternation of all Hindostan, the sentence was carried into speedy execution! The impression of the scene upon the people of India, though no doubt exciting emotions far more intense, was like what might be the general dismay of England, if some tyrannical king, who had subverted the Constitution, should undertake, without law, and upon some personal displeasure, to hang up the Archbishop of Canterbury. The prime minister of a prince, over whom the English certainly possessed no just control; respected and respectable for his priestly functions; universally known by reason both of his personal and political relations; entitled to some humane consideration, on account of his venerable age; he was shamefully dragged from his position as the public accuser of Hastings, arrested upon a charge generally believed to have been fictitious; under a law then recently adapted to the supposed commercial necessities of England, and which never was intended to have, nor could have any legal operation in Asia; for an offence, which we should regard it utterly unreasonable to make capital here, and which in India was considered as little criminal, as swearing to a false entry at the Custom-house in England,—this man, hemmed in by all the barriers and prejudices of rank, wealth, influence and religion, was publicly hanged at noon-day, amid the cries and tears of agonized millions, the victim of arbitrary and vindictive power!

It was for applying the term "murder" to this transaction, that Mr. Burke was subjected to the censure of the House of Commons. He received the announcement of their disapprobation, with that proud submission, correspondent to the whole course of his dignified and manly life. The state of feeling, which could be excited to the passage of such a vote, against their own authorized and noble manager, for even the strongest expression of indignant feeling, in pursuance of the duty which they had themselves imposed, amazes us now. But the statute, constituting forgery a capital crime, had been accorded, not long before, to the demands of the commercial community. The offence, a short time previously, had become more than usually common. Much excited feeling, as well as excited interest, had been stirred into action. Public sentiment, on this subject, was in a state of extreme exaggeration. Dr. Dodd had been executed, as a signal example, under this law, notwithstanding the most strenuous efforts in his behalf, headed by Lord Chesterfield, himself the injured party. But the House does not appear to have reflected, that a mere compliance with the forms of law could not constitute a justification for the conduct of Hastings. Its members did not stay to consider, whether Nuncomar was innocent or guilty; whether the forgery was a real or only a supposed case, or whether the offence, if proved, was punishable in Asia, as it was in England. Indeed, they did not investigate the question in its bearings at all. Mr. Burke had pronounced the execution of this man for alleged forgery, under all the extraordinary circumstances of the case, to be *murder*,—and this was enough to rouse the passions and prejudices of the day. No such censure could inflict a stigma upon its object. Of its reflective bearing upon the intelligence and purity of the tribunal, a different view might be presented. The statute has subsequently been repealed; and it is now well-understood law, that no English statute shall have power over the

Colonies, unless by express provision to that effect. To exhibit, in a strong light, the unreasonableness of the feeling alluded to, and the evils of partial and temporary legislation,—for this same offence, for which Dr. Dodd was sent to the gallows, near the middle of the last century, Dr. Bailey, another English clergyman, was transported to Botany Bay, within the past few years.

It is conceded by Mr. Macaulay, that "Impey, sitting as a judge, put Nuncomar unjustly to death, in order to serve a political purpose." But he palliates the conduct of Hastings, upon two grounds. First, that he might well consider "any means legitimate to his end, which were pronounced such by the sages of the law;" and secondly, that "Hastings cannot be blamed, for wishing to crush his accusers." They are both strange doctrines, and need but a brief reply. The "sages of the law," however, I may as well remark, were none other than Sir Elijah Impey, and him alone; and though such "sages" certainly have occasionally sat upon the bench, yet, to the honor of humanity be it spoken, they have not often been cotemporaries; but like other monsters, have appeared singly, and only at rare intervals, in the history of jurisprudence. The "political purpose," for which Impey put Nuncomar unjustly to death, was *the safety of Hastings*. The judge was his own creature, and the end was procured under his own influence and control,—and basely as Impey betrayed his trust, I have never yet learned that the tempted is more criminal than the tempter. Besides, the argument set forth, in palliation, is precisely the one employed by that ridiculous scarecrow, "Poor Peter Peebles," in the novel of "Red-gauntlet;" who protested it uncommonly hard, that he should be held amenable in conscience, for a most cruel and violent transaction of his more prosperous days, since all the proceedings in the premises were conducted *by due course of law*. That Hastings felt it for his interest "to crush his accuser," there can be no question. Men too often do such things, we know, and afterwards excuse themselves to their consciences, as well as they are able. Cromwell, under different circumstances, destroyed the adversary, who stood between him and his designs; and for this, of all his acts, the peace of Zimri was upon him to his dying day. But that a writer, professing a high standard of moral sentiment, should sit down deliberately in his study, to justify such an act, on such grounds, impresses one as really something amazing. Revenge and injustice, I trust, are not yet defensible propensities. However our conduct may fall short of our professions, we yet cannot forbear to hold ourselves accountable to higher considerations, of what is due to ourselves, to others and to the world—

Else wherefore breathe we in a Christian land?

If the accusations of Nuncomar were false, Hastings might well have defied them; if true, the honor of the British character demanded, that he should no longer disgrace his high official station. And to pretend, that either ruler or citizen, either for policy or security, may murder an open accuser, in order to prevent an investigation into his crimes, is a doctrine as novel in theory, as it would be terribly pernicious in fact.

But perhaps the crowning infamy of this man's misdeeds was the Rohilla war. It is the less necessary for me to enlarge on this topic, because in this instance, I believe, all are agreed to give up both Hastings and his country to merited disgrace. But I do not feel myself at liberty to pass it entirely by; especially as it may help to teach us, how some of those, who, in our day, are still reaping the pecuniary results of this bad enterprise, might find food for decent reflection nearer home, before they wasted such a profusion of cheap philanthropy abroad. The Rohillas were, by far, the most interesting people of India; brave, intelligent, cultivated, prosperous, hospitable and happy. They maintained their independence by their own courage, and stood secure, under a wise, prudent and paternal government. Their country is situated at the westernmost extremity of India, on the frontiers of Persia, separated from Hindostan itself by the river Indus; and through it runs that vast range of lofty mountains, which, commencing on the Mediterranean, under the name of Taurus, passes, by various denominations and in various directions, through the whole extent of Asia, to the sea of Okotsk and the Pacific Ocean in the east. It is styled, by an old writer, the "Paradise of the Indies." Agriculture and the arts of peace flourished throughout its fertile valleys; and the whole province presented a living realization of those golden days, sometimes found gliding away, in the nooks and corners of the world, to prove that, in elder times, the patriarchal age was not a pastoral fable. Without even the shadow of pretence, the Nabob of Oude, a tributary to the English power, and one of Hastings's intrusive governors, conceived the idea of annexing this rich territory to his dominions. He dared not make the attempt himself, for the Rohillas were warlike and to be feared; but negotiated with Hastings for assistance. For the sum of £400,000, and payment of the expenses of the war, Hastings was base enough to lend him the British bayonets. The Rohillas made every effort to avoid a conflict with the English, with whom they had no quarrel; but finding it impossible, put themselves upon their best defence. The particulars of the struggle are well worthy the closest attention. Be it enough for me to say, that, after a desperate and bloody contest, they were overpowered, and given up to the cruel mercies of the cowardly Nabob, who had fled while the combat was yet doubtful. His barbarities were so excessive, that the English officers sent to Hastings, imploring his interference; but he coldly declined to afford either command or advice, there being, as he alleged, no stipulation in the contract, as to the mode of conducting the war. Indeed, the Rohillas seemed to be almost exterminated. But the consequences of evil deeds do not slumber in the dust. The iniquities of the fathers are still visited upon the children, to the third and fourth generation. A scattered remnant of this brave and spirited people again gathered upon their native fastnesses; and a portion of their descendants, at least, are the same Afghans, who, on the same soil, within the past six or seven years, have taught England some of the most mortifying lessons ever imposed upon her military pride. I shall not undertake here formally to defend the Afghans, or their mode of conducting hostilities. Much is to be excused to a brave people, battling for their own rights, upon their native soil, against a powerful foe; especially when, as in the recent instance, the quarrel seems to have been as unreasonably fastened upon them, as in the old time. I suspect, if the truth were told, the invaders had little to boast about. One thing, however, is certain, that while the Afghans, on their part, exhibited to the captured ladies of the British officers a species of consideration and generosity, of which no memorials had been preserved for their instruction from the days of Sujah Dowlah,—the progress of the invading forces themselves emulated, if it did not surpass, every description of wanton cruelty, which defile the traditionary annals of the old Rohilla war.

I have endeavored, with a few necessary touches, to set forth, sufficiently for the purpose, those scenes, upon which Mr. Macaulay has employed all the gorgeous coloring of a vivid fancy and the utmost minuteness of pointed and picturesque detail. I should avoid undertaking to abridge, for recital, the heart-sickening atrocities of Dinagepore and its sister territories, for perhaps the same reason that they have been omitted by Mr. Macaulay. Besides the extreme horror of their revolting and most unnatural circumstances, upon the narration of this portion of the dreadful story Mr. Burke has expended all the luxuriant resources of his great and fertile mind. It would be difficult to do this subject equal justice with the rest, in the same degree that the language, the sensibility, the imagination, the comprehensiveness of Mr. Burke, are superior to similar faculties and qualities in any writer, who should attempt to follow him. Be it enough to state, that, in a province comparatively poor, it was a systematic, long-continued and most cruel effort, by a relentless agent, under the appointment and for the use of Hastings,—

> ——To wring
> From the hard hands of peasants their vile trash,—

executed with a dogged and perverse brutality, from which the very soul recoils almost incredulous,—and pursued, until every human pore, in the ill-fated territory, ran purple with the blood of agony; until age and infancy, and the shame and sensitiveness of woman, shrank from the demons, who defiled the nature of their own species, and laid themselves down in the jungle of the tiger and the hyena, rather than any longer endure the more savage intimacy of man. Whoever desires to recur more particularly to the voluminous materials, upon this subject, will find them fearfully set forth, in the fifth and sixth days' speech of Mr. Burke, at the opening of the impeachment.

These are but a few of the more marked and open exemplifications of the nature of British rule in India, during the last century. The infinite excesses and abuses, attributable to private corruption, it would be impossible to specify. The world has often wondered at the slow progress of the Christian religion in that region, and the apparently fruitless issue of missionary labors; and it has spoken of the impenetrable prejudices of the Hindoos, which, like threefold armor, rendered them alike indifferent to the spiritual sword, whether wielded by Jesuit or Churchman; whether the standard of the Cross was unfurled, upon the ramparts of Portuguese bigotry, or waved, where the doctrines, of which it was the sign, were enforced and illustrated by the more generous enthusiasm of a Heber or a Schwartz. But the early preachers of Christianity and their immediate successors, through difficulties and dangers now unknown, were able to overcome the most inveterate and diverse prejudices. The apostolic staff, if not always available for personal defence, was still their rod of support and comfort, as they traversed the most distant and inhospitable corners of the world. Upon stony places, by the way-side and among thorns, they flung the scattered seed; amidst the heritage of Ishmael, along the Idumean road,—and through this very India, into countries still more remote, where all traces of the specific worship have long since been swallowed up in the vortex of revolutions. As a curious and interesting exemplification of their primitive successes, the golden candlestick which they set up still glimmers, with a feeble light indeed, amidst the darkness of Ethiopia; and from the wild ranges of Kurdistan a Nestorian Bishop was, not long since, in this land, manifesting something of the traditionary simplicity of the ancient and original Church. But the truth is, the Hindoos had no sort of reasonable motive presented for their conversion. They were able to distinguish, to compare and to see. If they heard or read that precept of the Gospel, which, properly understood, lies at the very foundation of all Christian morality, which forbids us, as a chief good, to "lay up unto ourselves treasures upon earth,"—they had only to look about them and observe their Christian exemplars absolutely intent upon nothing else, and to this end devoting the whole energies and spirit of their lives. We know that commercial intercourse, governed by honorable principles and dignified and alleviated by higher considerations, is a useful, a necessary and a noble pursuit. But, unfortunately, the admitted standard of worldly morality is obviously far beneath the perfection of the divine requisition; and practices and principles pass more than current in the daily intercourse of society, which cannot be reconciled with the plainest obligations of duty. So thoroughly has the world settled the conditions of its law in opposition to the law of God, that the ordinary morals of business are too commonly anything but Christian morals. It is to be doubted, whether the moral conduct of Christendom compares favorably, in this respect, with that of many heathen nations. It is this fatal discrepancy between our professions and our practice, which unfits commerce to be the missionary of religion. As well expect Shylock to be converted by Antonio—and to anticipate the propagation of the Gospel amongst the simplest, much more amongst an intelligent and acute people, by means like these, would be as reasonable, as to look amidst the gray shadows, of the western horizon, on a wintry evening, for the matchless splendors of the summer dawn. If this be true, as a general rule, what successful progress could Christianity expect from a system like that of India, where all was fraud, all corruption, all cruelty, treachery and plunder? It resulted from these causes, no doubt, that the hopes of many were disappointed, because the influence and efforts of the English in China recently failed to exert any favorable tendency towards its civilization and conversion; and will still fail, thus presented, though medicined with—

——poppy *or* mandragora,
Or all the drowsy syrups of the world.

Indeed the refinements of civilization itself, if it be not elevated and controlled by a more spiritual power, seem to me to be, in reality, worse than the worst of all barbarisms. I cannot assent to the soundness of a much admired philosophical sentiment of Mr. Burke, (and it is not often that I should undertake to find fault with his philosophy) that "vice loses half its evil, by losing all its grossness." Mr. Burke was misled, by looking at vice abstractly, instead of by examples. A painted harlot may be, perhaps, more attractive, but is she less dangerous than her equal, in rags? The war-club of the African savage, which can be seen and avoided, is better than the stiletto of the more polished, but no less inherent barbarian, which secretly penetrates to the life. The soul of the untutored Indian, upon our Western prairies, true to all it has felt and known, is infinitely superior to the corrupt heart, that beat amidst all the splendid and hollow magnificence of the Roman Court. It is preferable that the mind should remain ignorant, and be so less potent for mischief, unless the heart becomes more and more purified, at every point of advancement in knowledge. It is impious to anticipate, that Heaven will favor the accomplishment of a good end, by evil means. Providence, no doubt, may interpose, to prevent the consequences of crime ; and leaving men equally responsible for their wicked purposes, may, in the exercise of supreme wisdom, benevolence and power, turn them all into an occasion of good. But this is the prerogative of God, and of Him alone! So far as we have reason to know, Providence does not see fit to encourage any hope of coöperation in our actions, unless they are prompted by commendable motives. For example and for punishment, it permits the natural return of those rewards, linked to our misdeeds by chains of inextricable adamant. Every principle of wisdom, every condition of moral necessity, requires the exercise of virtue for the attainment of virtuous ends. They afford us no warrant for supposing, that anything but evil can come out of evil, or that eventual benefit can be derived from anything but that which is in itself good. Our duty is, to be wise, prudent, virtuous, according to the measure of our capacity and opportunity; and we cannot safely say, that we will leave the consequences of our conduct to a higher Power, unless we have some good reason to be persuaded, that our motives and actions are in themselves right.

Indeed, the very spirit and constitution of Christianity forbid that we should expect such results, as have been anticipated, in India and China. Its first principle is *Peace*—how can you, therefore, propagate it with the sword! The very element of its system is *Love;* why should you, therefore, enforce it, with all the fiery malignity of hate?

I have left myself little space to remark upon the subsequent fortunes of Hastings. The conduct of affairs in India and the outrages of his administration had been, for several years, the subject of bitter dispute, at the Court of Directors and in the House of Commons. Although all things in England are more or less influenced by political bias, yet, in this instance, men, for a time, overleaped the barriers of faction. After an indignant vote of censure upon his conduct, in the House, it was resolved that he ought to be recalled. Soon after his return he was impeached; and the world has long rung with the fame of the celebrated orations of Burke, Sheridan and Fox, before that high tribunal, more august, it would seem, than competent, which sat in judgment upon his misdeeds. It has often occurred to my own mind, that, if Hastings could have been brought to the bar, for any single one of his many outrages, the general sense of humanity and justice, which governs deliberative proceedings in Great Britain, would have easily insured his condemnation and exemplary punishment. But the very multitude of his offences seems to bewilder and fatigue the attention; and the mind instinctively shrinks from believing, that any human being has been really defiled by such a complication of crimes. In him, it was a successive series of transactions, extending over a considerable space of time, and the traces of each separate enormity were obliterated, in his passive conscience, by the footsteps of its rapid successors; to us it is presented, as one vast and confused accumulation of horrors, from which we recoil incredulous, and are only too happy to escape their scrutiny.

For various reasons the trial was protracted, for a period of nearly eight years. In the mean time, vast changes had taken place. New political interests had sprung up. In regard to certain of them, several of the old opponents of Hastings had been irrevocably alienated from each other. Some of these had become connected with the ministry, which now took open sides with the Ex-Governor-general. Wherever art, influence, or money could avail with the press, the people or the parliament, they had been most zealously employed in his behalf. Public emotion had become very considerably allayed, and weariness had taken the place of indignation. Of the large body of peers, who sat in judgment at his impeachment, nearly one half had been themselves summoned to a higher tribunal. At the final judgment upon the charges, many of the Lords absented themselves ; and of about two hundred, then composing their body, only twenty-nine voted at all. Upon the vote of a majority of these he was eventually acquitted, in terms, by a singular sentence, which required him to pay more than £70,000, as a part of the costs of prosecution. If he were innocent, this was an unjust exaction,—if guilty, an infamous compromise. I am sorry to say that several of the most eminent in place, of the "spiritual Lords," voted for his acquittal, while amongst the "Lords temporal," who declared themselves for his condemnation, is to be observed, together with the names of others less known to us, that of the late venerable Earl Fitzwilliam, ever after distinguished for the unsullied integrity of his character, and the manly nobleness of his life. Whatever the offences of Hastings might have been, his administration of Indian affairs had added immense sums to the public revenues and the private fortunes of England ; and the estates of the wealthy aristocracy, of both

Houses, had been benefited, in many instances, directly or indirectly, by his means. His escape, therefore, was inevitable, for interest, not justice, held the unequal scale.

But the main immediate impediment to the rightful discovery of truth, upon this great occasion, was the determination, with which the Lords fettered themselves, that their investigations should be governed by the rules of evidence practised upon in the English Courts of Law. If it were becoming to say so, the absurdity, as well as the hindrance unavoidably occasioned by this resolution, must have pressed upon every step of their deliberations. This system of rules, in its own place, is not only wise and salutary, but absolutely essential to the despatch of business. It is necessary, both for the promotion of public justice and the security of private right. These rules are the result of great experience and sagacity. In the natural impossibility of framing such as could prove of universal application, their observance may often tend to the advantage of the criminal, and may sometimes save him from the just consequences of his crimes. But the enforcement of precision here is equally beneficial to the public, and the parties, interested in the event of each particular proceeding. To the public, because, without it, business would become embarrassed, trials interminable, law much more expensive, justice much more uncertain. To the party, because it secures him the assistance of competent persons, who have been led to investigate his rights and who know the strength of the defences, by which he is justly encircled and protected. At first sight, it may seem, for instance, a sort of refinement, to one who has not reflected on the subject, that a person, believed to have committed a capital offence, should be liable to be put on trial but once for his life. Yet when it is considered, that every man ought to have his offence clearly set before him, in order that he may meet it, if he can; and that, for the same reason, he ought to be proved guilty of that specific offence, before he shall be convicted,—it will be seen, that, while the public and the accused are saved from the burthen of repeated prosecutions, the accuracy of the proceedings, in every particular instance, is made of the greatest interest and consequence to all. And experience approves the wisdom of the theory. And it might be matter of grave reflection to some of our innovating law-givers, that, in fact, the subversion of substantial justice and the insecurity of legal rights will be always in exact proportion to that looseness of practice, which they have been so anxious to introduce.

But the matter, which we have been considering, was of a widely different nature. An Impeachment is an event of rare occurrence. Besides this, no instance had been known, in the experience of any of the parties engaged upon the occasion in question. The accused was one, by his position, constituted the vicegerent of a Power, by whom kings reign,—upon the broad principles of moral government, recognized and applicable, wherever the sun witnesses the beauty and excellence of his daily providence. The offences, with which he was charged, were crimes as well against the moral sentiments of mankind, as in defiance of the express provisions of the law. His accuser was the voice of humanity itself, which for fourteen years had echoed in the ears of his countrymen, across the vast ocean, which separates Asia from Europe. The tribunal, at which he was arraigned, was rather patriarchal than judicial in its functions; itself the source of all legislation and the supreme arbiter of right; and though, of course, amenable to the external law, yet in its own sphere, subject to no rules, except that wise discretion, with which the prudent and just man dispenses government to his own household. Much of the testimony was of that moral weight, which always avails and is enough, in the ordinary transactions, the intercourse and the business of society. The lookers on, in the great spectacle, were the civilized and the uncivilized world, all competent to determine upon the universal characteristics of inhumanity, oppression and fraud,—without confining themselves within those narrow limits of construction, held requisite at the Old Bailey or Petty

Sessions, in order to convict some half-starved culprit, of a breach of the game-laws, or half a shilling's worth of larceny.

Besides his most questionable services to his country's cause, (if that cause be such as honor and integrity may fairly sanction,) and his unprincipled extension of English jurisdiction by fraud and violence, not by wisdom,—there are, after all, two points in the character of Hastings, to which Mr. Macaulay directs his reader's attention. All personages, distinguished as he was, are known, of course, by certain marked characteristics of fortune and disposition. I venture to predict, that few would have been likely, in this relation, to hit, as Mr. Macaulay has done, upon the "want of rapacity" on the part of Hastings, and his "honorable poverty!" He asserts the Governor-general not to have been rapacious, because the whole sum and substance of his extortions were not devoted to his own individual benefit. But this was manifestly a thing impossible. Besides, there can be nothing more fallacious, than this mode of reasoning. In fact, few men care for money for itself alone. The character of a mere miser is as rare, as it is unamiable. The state of miserhood itself is as much a disease of the mind, as any of the other unfortunate hallucinations, to which human nature is subject. But men, in general, struggle for wealth, to secure the purposes of their pleasures and the gratification of their passions; for ambition, reputation, power; for the interest of their families, or to secure comfort for their own declining years; in short, to serve some kind of ulterior object, which the mere possession of wealth unemployed does not and cannot answer. Hastings knew that he could sustain himself in power, only by gratifying the cupidity of those who placed him there; and that he could eventually advance his personal objects, only by the same means. Mr. Macaulay excuses him, because, although he seized, without cavil, upon all the money he could grasp, he did not see fit to appropriate the whole to his own individual use; and urges, that he might have returned with a fortune, surpassing that of any crowned head in Europe. But Mr. Hastings was apparently wiser, in his day and generation, than to attempt any such quixotical undertaking. If he had done so, he would never have escaped condemnation. He remembered that he had other objects; that his conduct was closely scrutinized; that he had many and powerful adversaries, both in Europe and Asia; that he had been already, in effect, once displaced for abuses; that he had finally been summoned home from his government; that, in any event, in all likelihood, he would be called to strict private, if not public reckoning upon his return; that any flagrant and undisguised guilt, of this character, would deprive him of his only means of exculpation; that it would be more easily appreciable by his judges, less readily excusable by his immediate employers, since such a dazzling accumulation of plunder could have been kept for his own use, only at their expense;—and he contented himself with bringing home a fortune of only several hundred thousand pounds! His lady, indeed, had acquired a large additional and private treasure, by the same justifiable means,—without his connivance, says Mr. Macaulay,—but this could hardly be. His "honorable poverty" had been endured in India, during fourteen years, on a salary of £25,000, besides great opportunities. Moderation is undoubtedly a noble and an honorable quality; but I should hardly think of claiming it for that man, as a special virtue, who, having the chance presented of filling all his pockets with other people's money, contents himself with filling only one, on account of the difficulty of carrying the whole safely away. The bulk of the mutual acquisitions of Hastings and his lady was finally expended in conciliatory presents, and in the preparation for and conduct of the defence. His affairs fell into some confusion, and he was assisted with loans by the Company, who settled upon him eventually a sufficient pension. He regained his paternal estate of Daylesford, but the title was never revived in his favor. As one of the most striking instances, on record, of the caprice and injustice of popular opinion, when he was summoned to the bar of the Commons, in 1813, to give evidence relative to Indian affairs, the House, (that is, the successors of those, who once tried and virtually convicted him of high crimes and misdemeanors) rose and stood uncovered in his presence. Supposing him to have been only the doubtful character, which the most favorable history claims, it was to their indelible disgrace. Some of his old antagonists were still there. They pulled their hats over their brows, and kept their places.

It seems to have been matter of much occasional speculation in England, what were the real motives, which induced Mr. Burke to take so deep an interest in this great question, and to maintain, in regard to it, a position of such uncompromising and determined perseverance; or, to state the question in the only shape, which could make wonder on this subject justifiable,—for

— what stranger cause yet unexplored,—

so good a man as Mr. Burke could pursue with such unrelenting indignation so good a man as Mr. Hastings! I pass by the fact, that Sheridan and Fox, and others of high name, men of minds less pure and principles less sound than his, were with him, to a greater or less degree, in the progress of the prosecution. I omit also the consideration of the point, that a similar question, with all its attendant circumstances, seldom, if ever, has so forced itself upon the attention of mankind. Private hostility and a hundred other inadequate, improbable and unfounded motives have been suggested, to account for a course of conduct, which resulted from the clear qualities of Burke's character, and which lies upon the surface of the facts involved in the case. To the investigation of these he himself avers, that he brought the scrutiny, the reflection and the devoted and untiring labor of many years.

From all these supererogatory imputations Mr. Macaulay handsomely justifies him. He eloquently alleges that great man's intimate acquaintance with the history, government, manners, and all the public and private relations of the Asiatics. He supposes him to have been actuated only by the highest, the purest and most honorable considerations; but suggests the kind of coloring, with which his imagination invested the subject-matter, which he had so much at heart. The real question is, whether the Grand Inquest, thus summoned to serious duty, in the mind of Mr. Burke, did, in fact, "present things truly." And, indeed, this appears to have been the actual purpose, for which this much-abused faculty, this misunderstood imagination, was made part and parcel of the human character; to exhibit the distant, the past and the future,—things in which we have the highest interest, though they are remote and invisible, in their true aspect of real and absolute existences.

Without it, to some reasonable extent, heaven and hell, the absent and the lost, would be to us indeed unmeaning and most unsubstantial incomprehensibilities. The enjoyment of this faculty, unalloyed by selfishness or any baser interest or bias, enabled Mr. Burke to see things, precisely as they were to be apprehended by the mind, rather than the senses; to grasp the true character and bearing of events in India, just as if they had occurred at his own fireside. No doubt, it is the want of this quality, in some measure, which leaves men at a loss to account for the influences, which enabled him to see and to tell the truth. And it was this want, to a certain extent, combined with the thousand other easily-understood considerations, which led to the final discharge of Hastings. It is felt, as a great misfortune, sometimes, that criminals should escape, through the interests of men, or their incapacity rightly to appreciate what the purity of justice would require. But, in fact, if there were no Mr. Burkes in the world, or men of similar, if inferior characteristics, such persons would always escape, except so far as interest, vengeance, or some other private passion pursued them to doom. To cultivate and honor this quality, therefore, to every reasonable degree, would seem to be a sort of necessity of society, in order to raise and support what in it is low. For, as observation will teach us, that the mind of the individual man, when entirely devoid of imagination, scarcely comes up to the nobler instincts of many inferior animals,—so society, without a due intermixture of this temperament, by a certain natural and necessary consequence, becomes corrupted, degraded, selfish,—" earthly, sensual, devilish." For imagination is the handmaid of reason, as woman is the helpmeet of man,—and neither is capable of being compared with the other, upon any definite classification of their respective attributes; but the one continually serves the purpose of opening new vistas of immortal prospect, outside of the ordinary range of merely sensible thought, as the other equally inspires emotions, tending to the essential elevation of the human character, and which, otherwise, would lie sunken and undiscovered in the depths of the natural being.

I have spoken of the public history of Hastings, in a manner only too fully warranted by the ample evidence on record. It occurred to me to take up the subject in some detail, partly, because an article like that of Mr. Macaulay appeared capable of effecting considerable mischief, and partly, because I conceived it not inappropriate to the times to show, that all the sin of the world did not rest upon the consciences of the American people; and that, although it affords no apology for our own offences, yet, considering the extent and nature of the excesses committed, at no very distant period, in Asia, and excused if not approved by the legislative authority of England, the people of that country are not perhaps so much entitled, as if their skirts were clear, to fold their broad phylacteried robes about them, and to stalk away, justified, as if from some unholy contact.

And I do not admit the validity of the kind of defence, which is pretended to be set up for Hastings, by those who would palliate his conduct. A bad man may be made the instrument of bringing about some good, but yet he is a bad man. He, who with the power of doing unlimited evil, carries it only partly into execution, of course, is deserving of less severe condemnation, than one who is utterly and irretrievably depraved. But, in truth, the world affords very few examples of such monsters, for whom there is no means of urging some possibility of extenuation; and I know not where to look for them, unless, perhaps, under the Roman Empire, amongst several of the more tiger-like than human successors to the Julian purple. Yet if, on the tomb of Nero, some unknown hand strewed flowers, it ought not to surprise us, that apologists should be found for the enormities of Warren Hastings. In our moral judgment of men, since we are all only too frail and liable to temptation and error, it is surely becoming to exercise every reasonable degree of charity and fair interpretation. But when we cannot help perceiving an immense preponderance of evil, and that good or bad conduct alike are pursued only for selfish ends, it would be something more than weakness to bring to it either palliation or defence.

"His principles," admits Mr. Macaulay, "were somewhat lax. His heart was somewhat hard. We cannot with truth describe him either as a righteous or a merciful ruler. * * * Those who look on his character without favor or malevolence, will pronounce, that, in the two great elements of all social virtue,—in respect for the rights of others and in sympathy for the sufferings of others, he was deficient." One would think that this were enough! Unprincipled and hard-hearted, unrighteous and unmerciful! Regardless of other men's rights and unpitying towards their calamities! And being thus apparently out of the pale of those ordinary and necessary attributes of our nature, which both human and divine requirement make essential to a man, much more to a ruler, he did not deserve,—at least the kind of article, in which he has been incidentally eulogized by Mr. Macaulay.

To allege him to have been a statesman, in any just sense of the language, appears to me to be absurd. His successes, such as they were, may be sufficiently accounted for, on other principles. "The world," remarks Dr. Johnson, "has been long amused by the mention of policy in public transactions, and of art, in private affairs; they have been considered as the real effects of great qualities, and as unattainable by men of the common level. Yet I have not found many performances, either of art or policy, that required such stupendous efforts of intellect, as might not have been effected by falsehood and impudence, without the assistance of any other powers." What the best of statesmen are, upon the recognized principles of society, involves a definition of qualities, to which there is no parallel in the character we have been considering. He is no more entitled to the distinction of this name, than the other unprincipled and unscrupulous tyrants, who spread dominion over the defenceless by conquest, who awe the weak by power, and extend empire by violence, and are great, only because they are successful. What a statesman ought to be, it might perhaps, in these days, appear somewhat invidious to inquire. In England, to regard the interest, to maintain the liberty, to promote the happiness of all classes of his countrymen; to be less ambitious of foreign conquest, than of contented peace at home; to uphold justice, that first great law of earth and heaven; to encourage moderation, to repress jealousies, and by reasonable concession, to avert impending revolution—in India,—if Providence had called him to preside over the destinies of infinite millions of mankind,—by a liberal wisdom and a wholesome integrity; by the maintenance of those virtues, which men are bound to practise; by the exhibition of principles, whose acknowledged theory our conduct denies; by proving that truths of more than momentary importance weigh somewhat upon our minds; to show that we are indeed desirous of promoting instead of impeding the great purposes, for which the Almighty created and sustains the world,—the welfare and happiness of all his creatures—

Th' applause of listening senates to command,
The threats of pain and ruin to despise,
To scatter plenty o'er a smiling land,
And read their history in a nation's eyes.

And, if we are told, that this is only ideal,—never heard of in Calcutta,—never dreamed about in Downing Street, or at Washington,—it is only because Truth has become ideal, through the corruptions and abominations of political machinations; because modern usages have converted things, in their origin good, into the worst of evils; have debased politics, from being the noblest of sciences, into the meanest of arts; have made government a treachery and diplomacy a fraud.

Indeed, I am acquainted with no stronger instance, than the one thus presented, of the danger of reposing great trusts in the hands of men, whose minds have neither been subdued by religion, nor disciplined and controlled by learning. For while true religion tends to the repression of all false ambition, true learning elevates and directs that which is purest, by storing the mind with the generous and honorable precepts of those who have gone before. Besides discouraging the emotions of interest and vanity, it sets before us the highest examples of truth and virtue ; and he would be least likely to corrupt the manners or pervert the liberties of his country, who enters upon the scene of his duties, from the company of philosophers, orators and sages, and all who have best illustrated whatever is noble, disinterested and dignified in the character of man.

And yet Mr. Macaulay, in language both touching and beautiful, deplores that the dust, which Hastings had dishonored, did not find its last repose under the cloistered arches of Westminster Abbey ! And though a life of crime, even in high places, would seem deserving of no better doom than a death of infamy, and though Jezebel, (to use one of those scriptural illustrations, to which Mr. Macaulay is so partial) even a king's daughter, was eaten by dogs in the portion of Jezreel—yet, in 'this temple of silence and reconciliation' he would build a trophy to the memory of Hastings ; to point out to the ingenuous youth of England, how a bad man, under the sanction of the Church itself, can be honored in his monument, when honors are useless, except as instructions to the living ; to teach them, that, Spartan-like, they may steal, if, with a high hand and an unblushing front, they secure success in their villany; to confound the difference, never too broadly marked, in human eyes, between virtue and vice; to draw a veil of still more impenetrable darkness, before that light, never too effulgent, through a worldly medium, which helps us to discriminate between right and wrong!

Had he really been admitted into that sublime sanctuary of philosophers, heroes and poets, where, side by side, sleep the rulers of England, each one in his own place,—he might indeed have been welcomed by much society, well enough suited to such a guest,—the Tudor and the Plantagenet, 'the stern Edwards and the fierce Henries,'—and if equal merit had forever met with equal reward, amid the silence and nothingness, where all men finally sleep together in the grave, he might there have lain down in company with the grasping and perfidious John,—the bloody Mary,—Richard, the crafty usurper,—and him, perhaps, the worst, whose brutal and unmanly tyranny neither learning softened nor religion restrained,—and all they *from beneath* might have been *moved to meet him at his coming!* But if the guardians of the temple have no privilege to exclude delinquent royalty from its precincts, they might well scruple at affording such a consummation to the obsequies of Hastings. If much that is unworthy necessarily reposes in those solemn shadows; if they who are there, were not free from the errors, the failings, the vices of men,—at least, it is well they should be such, that the first suggestion of their names, the first aspect of their mausoleums should associate itself with something that is honorable, agreeable or praiseworthy, in the history of mankind. But there, where the first promptings of an ambition, commendable if it had been generous, dawned upon his youthful mind,—there, where, after the lapse of more than three quarters of a century, his somewhat frivolous old age submitted to the "inevitable hour,"—let him, who desires to honor the memory of Hastings, bend over his tomb, in silence and alone, amidst the solitary obscurity of the chancel of Daylesford.

ADDRESS

BEFORE THE

MASSACHUSETTS HORTICULTURAL SOCIETY

ON THE

DEDICATION OF HORTICULTURAL HALL, BOSTON,

MAY 15, 1845.

MR. PRESIDENT, AND GENTLEMEN OF THE SOCIETY:—

IT is a touching, and to some of you, perhaps, familiar incident, which is related of a celebrated English traveller,* whose genius and misfortunes have long closely allied him with every human sympathy. He had penetrated the interior solitudes of Africa, in pursuance of his first adventurous researches into that distant and mysterious land. He was in the midst of the vast deserts of a barbarous clime, hundreds of miles away from the very outskirts of civilization, and surrounded on every side by the beasts of the wilderness, and by men scarcely less ferocious. He had suffered every privation and every ill. He was alone in the dismal waste, with a worn and failing body and a sinking mind. It was while

* Park.

the chance of life appeared a thing almost too hopeless for conjecture, and a thousand natural emotions thronged upon his soul; while the present seemed to crowd into its narrow hour the accumulated memories of all the past, and offered him but the prospect of a miserable death upon the barren sands, for the home which he had left with such eager and buoyant expectations, and the loved and lovely things he might behold no more—it was at this moment of despondency and distress, that an object caught his eye, which, perhaps, from the heedless or the happy, would scarcely have attracted a passing glance. It was a small moss, of extraordinary beauty, in the process of germination; and, as he contemplated the delicate conformation of its roots and leaves, the thought forced itself irresistibly upon his mind, that the same bountiful and eternal Providence, which protected this minute but lovely object in obscurity so complete, and in the region of perpetual barrenness, could not be unmindful of one of his intelligent beings, the highest in the scale of natural creation, for whose use and benefit the system of visible nature was itself ordained. It was the reflection thus suggested which banished his despair, and nerved his heart to those renewed efforts, which secured his eventual return to his native land.

There could be no more striking illustration than this, of the benevolent order of the universe; which so often vindicates itself under circumstances apparently fortuitous, by demonstrating the purpose and value of those things, whose utility a cold philosophy had endeavored to discover in vain. It were, indeed, too much to say, that the minutest atom which floats in infinite space, or the meanest flower that blows upon the bosom of nature, has been created for no valuable end. If the purposes of existence were less than they really are, in the eye of reason and enlightened philosophy, we might have been subjected to a very different constitution of outward things. To surround us merely with those objects, which might minister to our actual necessities, were to deprive our senses themselves of their very noblest attributes, and to contract within the narrowest limits the circle of our capacities and desires. Take from us, indeed, those lovely manifestations of external beauty; those sweet, and graceful and glorious creations, which tend much more, perhaps, to the promotion of our present happiness, as well as to the perfection of our immortal destiny, than all which the world counts most worthy of its pursuit,—and our minds were dark, and our hearts dead within us, instead of kindling with the glowing earth, as, radiant with brightness and beauty, she smiles to meet the embraces of the returning Spring.

The very savage, indeed, must derive some moral elevation from the contemplation of external nature.

For his untutored soul, as well as for the mind of the most cultivated student of the works of creation, that orient pavilion, flushed with a thousand gorgeous and shifting hues, from whose refulgent portals issue the outgoings of the morning; the deepening loveliness of that softer heaven, which ushers universal nature to repose; the changing year, as its advancing seasons ripen into mellower beauty;—yes, all and each, within the rudest recesses of the primeval wilderness, as well as amidst the refinements of a more polished condition of life, in their turn have given wing to a sublimer imagination, have widened the sphere of intellectual exertion, and dignified the reflections and aspirations of the moral being. The Indian maiden, who decks her jetty tresses with the wild flowers plucked by the margin of the forest brook, drinks in from them the same images of grace, fragility and beauty, which they are fitted to inspire in the proudest bosom that beats in regal halls; where every silken tint that art has curiously embroidered, and every radiant gleam that glitters from clustered gems, were incomplete without these simpler charms, furnished by the cheap provision of nature, yet more resplendent in their freshness, than the array of Solomon in all his glory!

But if such be the universal influence of natural beauty; if over even the soul of a barbarian it exerts this inborn power to charm the imagination and elevate the mind; surely, amidst the hourly cares, which in more civilized life press upon the hearts of men, they can find no relief so easily attained, and, at the same time, so refreshing and salutary, as the contemplation of those lovely things, which our common mother, for the common use and entertainment of her children, hangs sparkling with dew-drops upon every tree, or flings with bounteous profusion over her luxuriant bosom.

Whoever enters upon the attentive examination of these objects, in the spirit of rational philosophy, will be certain to attain a reward at least commensurate with his exertions; for, if it acquire him no other possession, it cannot but bring him that priceless one, of an innocent heart and a gentle mind; and a student of nature, who should become sensual and debased, would present as strange an anomaly as an undevout astronomer.

Indeed, the constitution of the mind itself is imbued with the spirit of love for natural beauty. And sad were his lot, who has so entirely lost this impress originally stamped by the hand of God upon the soul of man,—who is so thoroughly "of the earth, earthy," as to have forfeited all conscious enjoyment of the glorious creation around him, crowned by every revolving season with its own peculiar magnificence and beauty. Of the tendency of many of the great pursuits of life to render us sordid and selfish, if they are modified by no controlling influence, the fact

16

is only too apparent. The very refinements of our social being corrupt as well as polish. The human character insensibly dwindles amidst the pursuits of civilized society. The range of our feelings becomes contracted under the weight of the conventionalisms of life. The sphere of thought itself grows narrower, in the plodding routine of daily occupations. Confined amongst the converging thoroughfares of populous existence, the man becomes almost necessarily assimilated, in thought and habit, to those with whom he is associated. He unconsciously conforms, and often degrades his being by conforming, to the settled maxims and theories around him ; until,

> Like a drop of water,
> That in the ocean seeks another drop,—

he confounds himself, and loses the identity of his own peculiar and perhaps nobler characteristics.

Consider, then, the mother of the seasons in some of her infinite manifestations. You wander into the fresh fields and gather the flowers of spring. In crystal vases, resting, it may be, upon sculptured marble, you cherish these frail children of the sun and showers. You renew them before they wither, and gaze with exquisite delight upon their delicate texture and the manifold perfection of their mingling hues. They appeal forever to your inmost heart, as silent mementos of all things sweet, and beautiful, and pure. They are eloquent of perpetual suggestions to the answering soul. They fill your mind more than all that lives upon the canvas of the mightiest master. The least and meanest of them all more satisfies your imagination, than the choicest statue wrought by the divinest hand. To your cultivated mind they address themselves, in their momentary beauty, like images of things more perfect in immortal loveliness. They are emblems of the affinities of your moral being with whatever is complete in infinite glory beyond the skies. Like the eternal stars, that, on the brow of midnight, assure us, with their unspeakable effulgence, that Heaven and its hopes are yet there, so these, the stars of earth, spring upon her verdant bosom, the mute memorials of an inscrutable immortality. In the humble dwelling-place of the poorest laborer, in some crowded city's dim alley, into which the golden light of day pours scarcely one beam of all his abounding and pervading flood, you may often discern some simple flower, which indicates the longing of our more spiritual being; which recalls to the mind's eye of the wearied man the green fields of his boyish days, and impresses him again and again,—oh, not in vain!—with the gentler and purer emotions of his childhood. They come upon him, amidst the dust and heat, and perhaps the wretchedness, of his daily lot, like outward manifestations of the inner spirit-world. They are the signals of thoughts

> Commercing with the skies.

They are like gleams of a fairer and brighter sunshine, from realms "beyond the visible diurnal sphere."

The time does, indeed, come to all men, when they would gladly escape from the crowd and confusion of common life, and

> Forth issuing on a summer's morn, to breathe
> Among the pleasant villages and farms,

would forget the thronging cares which have exhausted their hearts, in company with *the lilies of the field, that toil not, neither do they spin.* It is, indeed, by influences such as these that we acquire not only fresher impulses to duty, but far higher and nobler principles of action. Experience, it is true, teaches us that the mere drudgery of rural pursuits can have little effect, in raising the private or social condition of the man. To turn the verdant soil, for the mere sustenance of life, would as little impress his mind with the true sentiment of his occupation, as any poetical idea of the gloomy grandeur of ocean enters into the soul of the tempest-tost and weather-worn mariner. The rustic laborer might forever follow his plough upon the mountain side, and trample with heedless foot upon the brightest flowers, that appealed with dewy eyes in vain to his plodding sensibilities; and the village maiden, obeying those truer and nobler instincts, inseparable, I believe, from every woman's heart, with every returning Spring, might gather and weave them into her rustic coronal, with no definite consciousness of their more spiritual import. But to fulfil their highest ministry they must have become blended with their kindred associations. They must have linked themselves, as they have done, with the domestic, and public and religious story of the world. Their sweet and gentle names must have floated upon the voice of song. They must have given language of eloquent significance to the passionate impulses of the human heart. They must have spoken of the fragility of life, under that sweetest and most touching of all sad similitudes,—a fading flower. They must have crowned the wine-cup, amidst the revels of "towered cities," and mingled with the sunny locks of the queen of May, upon the village green. They must have waved upon the brow of the returning victor, wreathed their modest tints amongst the tresses of the blushing bride, and reposed in pale and tranquil beauty upon the marble bosom of death. They must have proved their power to sound the secret well-springs of our hearts, and to draw up the sweeter waters beneath, hidden, as with a veil, by the intertangled sophistications and falsehoods of the world. They must have been won from their wild and unseen solitudes, and nurtured and cherished with a dear and reverent love.

But much as we love to meet them in their green retreats, on the fragrant meadow, by the rural roadside, or in the wild recesses of the rocks, it is as the friends and companions of our daily duties, that we most welcome their sweet and holy ministry. Nurtured by our own hands, they become indeed the faithful solace of our cares, and the rich reward of all our pleasant toil. And then, how more than strange is this wonderful result with which beneficent Nature repays our fostering charge! What miracle so marvellous, as this mysterious development, which we so disregard, because we call it the common course and order of creation! When the returning season fills our hearts anew with its returning hopes, we take the unsightly and insignificant seed. We bury it out of our sight beneath the dark, insensate earth. The dews and the showers fall upon what might well seem to be its eternal bed. The sun reaches its secret resting place with a vital and incomprehensible energy. It awakens from its slumber, and no apparent elements of its original conformation remain. It starts into being, developing newer and ever-varying aspects, —till

> from the root
> Springs lighter the green stalk, from thence the leaves
> More aery, last the bright consummate flower
> Spirits odorous breathes.

And then, what human philosophy is competent to explain the unseen cause, which, from elements apparently so inadequate, brings up the slender and tapering shaft, shoots forth the verdant leaf, and embellishes its lustrous crown with inimitable purple, or the flowering gold! What wonderful chemistry is this, which so filters the moisture of the earth and the dew of heaven, and combines and diffuses the just proportions of the vital air through every intricate fibre, till it blushes in the bloom of the queenly Rose, and makes the virgin Lily the emblem of purity and light! With what unerring skill they are blended or contrasted, in their infinite variety of "quaint enamelled dyes"! With what exquisite order and precision their gorgeous retinue appears, each at its accustomed season, and gathers the successive harvest of its transient glory!

Daffodils,
That come before the swallow dares, and take
The winds of March with beauty; violets dim
But sweeter than the lids of Juno's eyes
Or Cytherea's breath; pale primroses,
That die unmarried ere they can behold
Bright Phœbus in his strength; * *
* * * bold oxlips, and
The crown-imperial; lilies of all kinds,
The flower-de-luce being one.

Of all the gentle and welcome company, not one but lifts its starry cup or hangs its clustering bells upon the spiral stem. And oh, still stranger transformation, when this treasured darling of an hour, so rich in glowing charms and fragrant with delicious sweetness, yields to the immutable law of its destiny, refolds the vital principle of its being within the shapeless and scentless husk, and flings itself once more to its wonted repose in the embraces of the fulfilling earth!

It were, perhaps, too much to allege, that for our use and pleasure alone were created these loveliest objects of the natural world, so curious in contrivance, so matchless in surpassing beauty, so eloquent in the lessons of unerring wisdom. Of the originally perfect, but now interrupted, relation between things beautiful and things morally good, we may form some not irrational conjecture. That they are sadly disjoined, under our present condition, we well know. But if, as we are told,

> Millions of spiritual creatures walk the earth,
> Unseen, both when we wake and when we sleep,—

it were not unreasonable to conclude, that, to their celestial apprehension, the lovely aspects of creation may afford a delight correspondent with the primal relations between all things in themselves excellent; that to them, as to the Infinite Author, the loveliness of creation may seem *very good.* Nor are we capable of understanding, how far the inferior orders of being are susceptible of enjoyment from the same sources with ourselves. That their organs are affected to some extent by the same sights, as well as sounds, which address themselves to our own sensations, and that they do appreciate some of the properties of the vegetable world, we have the most abundant evidence. That the "grazed ox" would trample, in the fragrant meadow, upon the springing blossoms, that fill the soul of the merest child with irrepressible delight, is no less true, than that the bee lingers upon the flowery bank, in pursuit of his sweet repast, or that the wild bird trills his spontaneous song where dews are brightest, amongst leaves and flowers. Yet we may be sure, that to us alone, of the common dwellers upon earth, is given the power of justly appreciating these munificent gifts of the benevolent Author of all things. To us alone has been afforded the faculty of deriving the most innocent enjoyment from their cultivation and care; and, since the first habitation assigned to our common parents was indeed a Paradise,* we may conclude, that in the indulgence of no other of our pleasures do we so nearly approach their happy and sinless state.

There can be, indeed, scarcely a change more striking, than to leave the noisy streets of the "dim and treeless town" for the pleasant garden, stretching away under the broad reviving sunshine, in the sweet

* ΠΑΡΑΔΕΙΣΟΣ, a garden.

and open air. Of all the ordinary vicissitudes of life, I am aware of none which involves a revolution so absolute. We quit the sights which offend us at every turn, and enter upon a scene affluent in all things, which please the eye and refresh the imagination. Instead of the tumult and intemperate haste of the crowded haunts of men, we rest with the repose of nature, broken only by murmurs that are delicious, and the warbled music of the skies. For the suffocating steam of crowded life, we inhale ineffable perfumes, that float upon the breath of flowers. We forget the debasing competitions of wealth and fame, and enter into the innocent pursuits of the guileless creatures of the air. Instead of the too often profitless companionships of society, we meet ourselves. We become the companions of our own inner thoughts, and the things which intervene between our hearts and heaven are those, which only link us more closely to the infinite aspirations of our souls. That voice within speaks to us like a trumpet, whose whispers were almost inaudible through the tumult and hurry of life. The heart which was harder than the nether millstone, in the cave of Plutus, softens and expands to the just amplitude of its nature, beneath the liberal sunshine and under the broad and bounteous atmosphere. And still, like that primal Eden, though shorn and diminished of those heavenly flowers,

That never will in other climate grow,

it is yet the faint image of the original paradise, and the only earthly region instinctive with the spirit of an Almighty and universal Love. For here, indeed, it is that

> ——— o'er the flower
> His eye is sparkling and his breath hath blown,
> His soft and summer breath, whose tender power
> Passes the strength of storms in their most desolate hour.
>
> A populous solitude of bees and birds
> And fairy-form'd and many-colored things,
> Who worship him with notes more sweet than words,
> And innocently open their glad wings,
> Fearless and full of life; the gush of springs,
> And fall of lofty fountains, and the bend
> Of stirring branches, and the bud which brings
> The swiftest thought of beauty, here extend,
> Mingling, and made by Love, unto one mighty end.

It is from places like these, that the benefactors of the world have derived the strength of their generous impulses. It is here that statesmen and poets and philosophers have retired, and moulded those divine conceptions, which have resulted in the advancement and elevation of mankind. It was into such a retreat, that that noblest Roman,* styled by one† "the most wise, most worthy, most happy and the greatest of all mankind," entered, after he had made his native city the mistress of the world. In that venerated solitude, to which many a pilgrim step turned, in the succeed-

* Scipio. † Cowley.

ing ages of his country's history, wiser than he who, in later times,

Exchanged an empire for a cell,—

he forgot alike his glories and their cares, and conceived that illustrious sentiment, which could never have arisen in an ignoble or ambitious mind, *Nunquam minus solus quàm cùm solus.* From the rose-beds of Pæstum, rich in the bloom of their double harvest,* was wafted that breath of flowers, which ages ago stirred and mingled with the sublimest of human emotions in "Rome's least mortal mind:" from that Pæstum, whose fragrant odors yet faint upon the summer gale, amidst the ruins of man's less durable achievements; that Pæstum, where still

The air is sweet with violets, running wild
Mid broken pieces and fallen capitals;
Sweet as when Tully, writing down his thoughts,
Those thoughts so precious and so lately lost,
(Turning to thee, divine philosophy,
Ever at hand to calm his troubled soul,)
Sailed slowly by two thousand years ago,
For Athens; when a ship, if northeast winds
Blew from the Pæstan gardens, slacked her course.

We have read, with ennobling emotions, in our school-boy days, of the reluctance with which the royal gardener of Sidon † left his pleasing toils, for

* Biferique rosaria Pæsti.—Virg.
† Abdolonymus.

the purpose of assuming the burdensome cares of state. And it was from such a scene that Horace might well have refused to part, to enjoy the more intimate companionship of the master of the world; especially as this doubtful privilege must have been alloyed with the society of that proud but degenerate capital, to which Jugurtha, not long before, had said adieu in language far more just than flattering: "Farewell, O cruel and venal city, which requirest only a purchaser, in order to sell thyself and all which thou dost contain." And it was in the shades of those Salonian gardens, which his own hands had made, that Diocletian, the emperor, received the ambassadors, who vainly strove to reïnvest his brows with

> the hollow crown
> That rounds the mortal temples of a king.

But perhaps one of the finest natural illustrations of the interest, which still clings to pursuits like these, long after the heart is comparatively dead to all other human cares, is to be found in the pages of the great novelist, whose pictures appear to us less like efforts of imagination, than delineations of nature herself in her invariable aspects. The venerable Abbot of St. Mary's, according to the tenor of the tale, formed apparently for times less troublous than those which then distracted his unhappy country, resigns to a bolder spirit his conspicuous post in the van of the armies of the church, now become literally and carnally militant. He betakes himself, with cheerful resignation, to the horticultural occupations of his earlier and happier days. But his present pursuits, as well as his former condition and character, serve to involve him in the plots and counterplots, formed for the liberation of that fairest flower of Scotland's beauty, whose uttered name has so long awakened, and will forever awaken, every romantic emotion in the human bosom ; of that lovely Mary, less a queen than a woman, whose melancholy story, after the lapse of nearly three centuries, so stirs the heart, that all seems harsh and cruel, which sullen history would dare to blend with the memory of her beauty and her wrongs. Yet in spite of her loveliness and misfortunes, the pious and transmuted Abbot, stricken, it is true, somewhat into the vale of years, struggles hard between his allegiance to his queen, consecrated, as it is, by his duty and devotion to the church, and his affection for his garden-plots, which the rude feet of messengers and soldiers might trample ; for his fruits and his flowers,—his bergamots, his jessamines and his clove-gilliflowers. Let queens escape from prison, or kingdoms pass away, so the season return in its freshness to his more intimate domain. "Ay, ruin follows us everywhere," said he ; "a weary life I have had for one to whom peace was ever the dearest blessing. * * I could be sorry for that poor queen, but what avail earthly sorrows to a man of fourscore?—and it is a rare dropping morning for the early colewort."*

But I know of no picture more agreeable than that of old age, which the world, if it has robbed it of all things else, has been unable to cheat of its relish for these innocent pleasures. There is nothing to rival it, unless it be the unalloyed delight of children, in the midst of a garden. How eagerly they scamper along the walks, and stoop over the brightening beds! At the very approach of spring, their hearts are bounding as at some unheard-of joy. To them, the golden hours of summer are laden with a rapture unknown to later years. With what exquisite enjoyment they enter upon the minutest examination of the most common things! The flowers that are their own make them rich with an almost untold wealth. The springing grass to them is like the verdure of a fairy creation, and every folded bud comes forth, the miracle that it is in their soft and earnest eyes.

And then, what a host of illustrious names throng upon our memories, and seem to sanctify these pleasant and quiet scenes. I speak not now so much of the poets, who have been forever the chosen interpreters of nature's mysteries, and wanting whom, she might forever have uttered oracles, sounding to the wise, but vague and indefinite to the general appre-

* The Abbot, Vol. II.

hension. But the time would fail me to tell the great and illustrious names of English history, blended with every memory of these endearing pursuits: of Wolsey, magnificent in all his enterprises; of Sidney, conceiving the delicious dreams of "Arcadia," in his ancestral bowers at Penshurst; of Wotton, flattering the Virgin Queen with his present of orange trees from Italy, still flourishing in their original perfection; of Temple, whose heart so clung to the delightful recreations of his leisure hours, that, by his will, he directed that heart itself to be buried beneath the sun-dial in his garden; of Evelyn, whose very name awakens every pleasing association connected with rural pursuits, and whose noble sentences are full of the heart and soul of one, who loved the soil that bore him, with every emotion becoming a patriot and a man; of Raleigh, the graceful and gallant, learned and brave; of Bacon, in the language of Cowley,

> Whom a wise king and Nature chose
> Lord Chancellor of both their laws;

of that Bacon, who would have fresh flowers upon his table, while he sounded the depths of divine and human philosophy; of Addison, the regenerator of a more manly taste in gardening, as well as literature; of Locke, the childlike philosopher, exchanging his researches amongst the labyrinths of the human mind for studies on a fairer page, the open book of Nature, in her

> hues,
> Her forms, and in the spirit of her forms—

and who, unlike that illustrious Roman, to whom I have referred, loved the society of children rather than perfect solitude ; of Cowley and Pope, Walpole, Shenstone and Cowper, and a hundred others, who have illustrated this subject by their genius, and who are dear to us by every kindred tie which connects us with the memorials of the mind ; of Newton, conceiving, from a natural phenomenon in his garden, of the mighty law which balances this solid earth amidst the unshaken spheres ; of Fox, turning without a sigh from that great assembly which he had so often controlled by his sagacious eloquence, and finding, amidst his flowers and trees at St. Anne's Hill, a happiness far more real, than during the long years, when he had been the very idol of popular applause, or for the brief but dazzling hour, when, having finally grasped the prize of a life-long ambition, he directed the destinies of millions of his fellow men ; or of Washington—our own—the greatest name of all—forgetting, amidst rural pursuits and pleasures, every care, but that never-ending anxiety for the welfare of his country ; while the gathering plaudits of the grateful people, blessed under his beneficent rule, swelled above the retreating echoes of victory,—until all grew at length to him inaudible, amidst that hallowed repose, and beneath the solemn whispering shadows of Mount Vernon.

And oh, what glory and delight have the poets flung around these delicious resting-places of the soul!—from the time of the wise and royal singer of Israel, who tells us, "I made me gardens and orchards, and I planted in them trees of all kind of fruits;"* from the father of Grecian minstrelsy, revelling in fancy in the gardens of Alcinous, and the master of the Roman lyre, learned in all the science of the generous pursuit; from the sylvan shades of Arqua, and every "bosky bourne" which Boccacio so exquisitely delineates, down to the grottoes and flower-beds of Twickenham, and the almost sacred solitudes of Olney. With what a charm the imagination insensibly clothes the passage of those golden hours,

When Jonson sat in Drummond's classic shade!

What tree of our own planting is more familiar to us than Pope's willow, or Shakspeare's mulberry, set by himself in his garden at New Place? And we have all of us, I trust, devoutly execrated the barbarous hand, which so recently despoiled this tree of trees, which, but for such sacrilege, might have been visited by our children's children. And when we read, in one of the early biographies of Milton, that "a pretty

* Ecclesiastes.

garden-house he took in Aldersgate street, at the end of an entry, and therefore the fitter for his turn, by the reason of the privacy, besides that there were few streets in London more free from noise than that;"* we may well believe that there, rather than in the shock of life, his serene imagination might lavish all its riches amongst the flowery groves of Paradise. Yes! it is the true poets who are with us, not only when the sunshine nestles upon the mossy bank or beds of violets, but who come to us alike when Nature herself is sad and silent, and, even at the wintry fire-side, pour the joy of summer into our longing hearts. It is they who have embroidered the virgin page with inwrought words of every curious hue,—

> Of sable grave,
> Fresh green, and pleasant yellow, red most brave,
> And constant blue, rich purple, guiltless white,
> The lowly russet, and the scarlet bright;
> Branched and embroidered like the painted Spring;
> Each leaf matched with a flower, and each string
> Of golden wire; * * * *
> * * There seem to sing the choice
> Birds of a foreign note and various voice;
> Here hangs a mossy rock; there plays a fair
> But chiding fountain purled; not the air
> Nor clouds, nor thunder, but are living drawn;
> Not out of common tiffany or lawn,
> But fine materials which the muses know,
> And only know the countries where they grow.

* Phillips.

Without these glorious hues and forms, indeed, I know not of what materials the literature of a nation could be composed. And thus it is, that from the earliest age, and amongst every people, their beauty and the spirit of their beauty have haunted the soul of song. We know that, in all the countries of the East, flowers have forever constituted the symbols of sentiment and affection. The Greeks, who appear to me by no means deficient in that element of the romantic, which the moderns are so ready to arrogate entirely to themselves, were passionate in their love of flowers. From them have descended to us the custom of their employment in triumphal pageants, and on occasions of joyful or mournful ceremony; and they had scarcely a familiar flower, of the garden or the field, which their imagination had not woven into some lovely legend, or made the subject of some fanciful metamorphosis. By that most poetical of all people, the Hebrews, they were employed as the vehicles of many a touching and beautiful similitude. Of all the gorgeous company, there are none so familiar to our tongues and hearts, as the two which they have most distinguished with their affectionate admiration. How the spirit of devotion itself appears to spring, at the very mention of those well-known names of things so beautiful and pure!

By cool Siloam's shady rill
  How sweet the Lily blows;
How sweet the breath, beneath the hill,
  Of Sharon's dewy Rose!

I have thus endeavored, gentlemen, to discourse to you in a manner, I would fain hope, not entirely inconsistent with the spirit of the occasion. It has been my purpose to avoid that turn of technical remark, which, before such an audience, might have proved presumptuous in me rather than instructive to you. That scientific knowledge, which the genius and enterprise of modern times have brought to the pursuit of your liberal objects, may be found in sources easily accessible. Of the dignity and value of these objects it were unnecessary to speak. To apply any elaborate eulogium to this pursuit were as reasonable, as to justify the great sun of Heaven himself, in the fullness and glory of his illustrious beams. The beautiful and costly edifice, which you have erected, is the most fitting testimonial of your liberality, as its purpose affords the surest evidence of a refined and intellectual community. "God Almighty," says Lord Bacon, "first planted a garden; and indeed it is the purest of human pleasures; it is the greatest refreshment to the spirits of man; without which buildings and palaces are but gross handiworks; and a man shall ever see, that, when ages grow to civility and elegancy, men come to build stately, sooner than to garden finely; as if gardening were the greater perfection."

There can be, indeed, no question whatever that Horticulture, as a scientific pursuit, is of very recent date. The most famous gardens of antiquity, we may be sure, could enter into no sort of comparison with those, which would now be considered as exhibiting the most moderate pretensions, in point of the variety and beauty of their productions. As to what those were, with their arbors, which Cæsar bequeathed to the Roman people, we can form little adequate idea.* The hanging gardens of Semiramis have been accounted amongst the wonders of the world. Yet nothing can be more certain than that the "Beauty of the Chaldee's excellency" could afford the royal mistress of Assyria not a single nosegay, to be compared with the meanest of those, which constantly grace your elegant and spirited exhibitions. Were it not for the apparent necessity of the case, arising from the absence of intercommunication between different people, it would be unaccountable how little progress was made, for long ages, in an art so eminently attractive in itself, and so universally interesting to mankind. It is true, that conquerors, at all periods of time, have traversed vast portions of the world. But, with the exception of the emperor Napoleon, the pursuits of science, or the advancement of society, have rarely entered into their schemes of personal or national aggrandizement. But what vast improvements in this, as in other respects, have resulted from the extending commerce of the world!

* Cæsaris hortos.—*Hor.*

Of all the countless profusion of fruits and vegetables, which make the fertile face of England "as the garden of the Lord," those indigenous to her soil are of the most insignificant description. Few even of those sweetest flowers, which her later poets have woven into many a golden song, are of her own original production. The oak, and some of the more common forest trees, were all that her Druid groves could boast. The very mulberry of Shakspeare was, in his day, a rare exotic, and one of a large importation procured from the continent by King James, in 1606. And if, as we are told, in the times of Henry VII., apples were sold at one and two shillings each, the red ones bringing the best price, we may conclude, that when Justice Shallow treated Falstaff to a *last year's pippin of his own graffing*, it might be an entertainment, at least, commensurate with the dignity of such a guest.

It has been recently stated, that the average value of the plants, in a single horticultural establishment of London, is estimated at a million of dollars. And oh, before this magnificent result had been reached, from the comparatively trifling beginning, of a few centuries ago, what infinite care and cost must have been expended; what love for the generous science must have been fostered and encouraged; what distant and unknown regions had been visited and rifled of the glories of the plains and woods!—from solitary Lybian wastes and those paradises of Persia, the Land of Roses, so eloquently described by Xenophon; from

> Isles that crown th' Ægean deep,

to the boundless expanse of this bright heritage of ours; from Tartarian deserts to prairies of perpetual bloom; from the fertile breadth of fields, beneath the southern skies, to the strange continents of foreign seas and verdant islands of the ocean,

> ——— whose lonely race
> Resign the setting sun to Indian worlds.

Combined with this adventurous spirit of modern discovery, is another principle, which has proved eminently favorable to the interests of horticultural science. The higher social condition of those softer companions of our garden-walks and labors and gentle cares; the more liberal position awarded them, under the influence of advancing civilization; our deeper interest in their moral and intellectual culture, and our more generous regard for their innocent gratification, have entwined a thousand graces and refinements, once unknown, amongst the coarser texture of social life. Never, indeed, do they enter so intimately into our joys, and griefs, and affections, as in gardens and amongst flowers. For them, and not for ourselves, we reclaim the scattered blossoms along the wilderness of Nature; we ask of them a more tasteful care in the cultivation of these sweet and beautiful objects, thus won from the desert and a thousand times rewarding all our pains; and for their pleasure and adornment we mingle those softest, brightest hues, and fold the interwoven bud and flower and leaf into innumerable shapes of grace and loveliness.

Welcome, then, for this, if for no other cause, the Hall which you have thus prepared, and have decorated and garlanded to-night with the choicest treasures of the Spring. Long, long may it stand, an evidence of no vain or idolatrous worship. Unlike those *grosser handiworks* of cold and glittering marble, which crowned, in ancient days, the barren cliff, or looked, in lifeless beauty,

> Far out into the melancholy main,—

but touched with the spirit of every gentle and noble association, and consecrated by the soul of all our dearest affections, welcome, to them and to us, be this Temple of the Fruits and Flowers.

EULOGY ON PRESIDENT TAYLOR,

AT THE

OPENING OF THE CIRCUIT COURT OF THE UNITED STATES, IN BOSTON, JULY 15, 1850.

MAY IT PLEASE THE COURT :—

I RISE, with feelings of inexpressible sorrow, to perform the severe and mournful duty, which my position imposes upon me. I announce to you, officially, that sad event, which has already become known to you through so many channels, the sudden and lamented decease of Zachary Taylor, President of the United States. It is well that some brief interval has taken place, between the occurrence of this great national calamity and the session of the Court. Our minds required the indulgence of some lapse of time to enable us to recover, in a measure, from the first shock of an affliction so profound ; and that we might regain some power of language, in which to interchange the painful emotions of our hearts.

It is little more than one brief year since General Taylor assumed the exalted station, which He, who holds the lives of all men and the destinies of nations in his hands, has called upon him thus unexpectedly to relinquish. To that station he was welcomed by the unbounded confidence of his friends and the sincere respect of his opponents; and the whole people regarded him with that involuntary admiration, which his signal success in the field had excited in the hearts of this nation, and in the eyes of the civilized and uncivilized world. For there is no remote people, amongst whom the flag of our country has been unfurled, which has not heard of his triumphs, and learned through them to respect the American name.

His wisdom, his moderation and his sterling worth had allied to him more strongly, every day, the affectionate trust of his fellow-citizens. At a period of great doubt and perplexity and danger, in the affairs of this country, they reposed securely upon his sagacious counsels and the undoubted purity and integrity of his heart. And in every crisis his honored name would have been as a tower of strength, around which to rally the great energies of this nation, for the maintenance of whatever is dear to us in the institutions and inheritance of our fathers.

It has pleased God to disappoint these expectations; and he who was yesterday our hope, is mingled to-day with the common and undistinguishable dust. The language which faltered from his dying lips will form the noblest and most appropriate epitaph for his tomb: "*I am not afraid to die. I have endeavored to perform my duty. My only regret is in leaving my friends.*" Like whatever else he has uttered, upon the eve of great occasions, it embodies, in brief and forcible expression, those striking elements, which constituted the admirable basis of his character; his deep affection, his devotion to duty, his trust in God, and that high courage, which had so often sustained him in the face of the enemy, and now indeed has proved unfailing to the last.

For himself, his death is happy, glorious and august! He was at the summit of human greatness. He had sought no such elevation; and all men felt that, in his administration of his great office, no selfish feelings or purposes could intermingle. He was blessed by the entire devotion of domestic attachment; and,

> Honor, love, obedience, troops of friends

accompanied him, with unfaltering adherence, in the exalted course of his daily life. He has now escaped, by death, those vicissitudes which attend upon the highest earthly estate. Envy, detraction, and the force of all those miserable passions, which too generally influence the conduct of mankind—

> Malice domestic, foreign levy, nothing
> Can touch him further.

He has left to his country a name and an example, worthy the glorious days of the noblest republic in the most heroic age. He has died amidst the general and heartfelt grief of his fellow-citizens. And it is not too much to say, that no public man, in this or any other nation, has ever left the scene of his mortal labors, amidst the more universal sorrow of all classes and conditions of the people. Were this the fitting time and place for the expression of such feelings, I might well speak more at length of the almost filial veneration, with which many, who had been favored with his personal intercourse, regarded him. But the language of private grief it is scarcely becoming to mingle with the voice of public and general lamentation; and all, who can appreciate such a character, have the right and the privilege to claim their share in the common loss. For he was eminently one, who aspired only to be the father of his country; and earnestly he strove to emulate the virtues and patriotism of him, whose name has long since been consecrated by the universal homage of mankind.

Assuredly I have read in vain the history of the world, and have failed to regard with justice the character and conduct of my cotemporaries, if I err in believing, that the late President of the United States possessed, in a singular degree, the true elements of unquestionable greatness of character. We may, indeed, indulge in vague notions of human superiority; and while the mind is dazzled by this ideal standard, few whom we have known, and, it will prove, that few whom the world has ever known, will come up to our delusive criterion. But, reduce human nature in general to the sad, yet true proportions of its qualities, and there are few, indeed, whose many virtues and slight counterbalancing frailties will leave them so far above the level, as he whose loss we now so sincerely deplore.

For the mind of the President was capable of the highest conception of what constitutes the common good, and his heart included in its broad embrace every object of the most enlarged benevolence. His fervent and devoted patriotism, bounded by no barrier of education or prejudice, was ready to undergo the extremest sacrifice for the public welfare. He exhibited a firm reliance, in the darkest hour, upon the tried resources of his own resolution and judgment, an unshaken constancy of purpose, a superiority to evil fortune, and serene moderation under the more dangerous advances of the best—a true and exact integrity within every public and private relation—and to unblemished purity of life he joined the most unassuming simplicity of demeanor, and that dignified humility, which is a jewel of untold price upon the brow of the ruler of the people. A long and prosperous course of existence, so spent in the service of his country as to conduct him, eventually, without solicitation, and against his well-known desires, to be the leader and chief magistrate of more than twenty millions of freemen, ended in an administration of affairs, which, meeting and conquering many scruples and prejudices, has won for him the affection and veneration of the people, until now, that they weep no simulated tears, as his gray and honored head is laid in the common dust. And if qualities, and purposes, and successes, such as these, do not constitute the highest claims to human greatness, I am at a loss where to look for them in the history of mankind.

The Roman poet, in an age full at least of the memory of heroic qualities and characters, has set forth his model of a great ruler as

"Justum et tenacem propositi virum;"

and claiming this noble and admirable description, we can yet embellish its very justice in its application, when we proclaim that General Taylor was eminently a *true* man,—true to himself—true to all mankind; that he never did intentional wrong to any human being; but devoted his whole life, with all its most honorable purposes and energies, to the welfare of others and the promotion of the common cause.

That great biographer of the wonderful men of antiquity, whose pages he loved to study and contemplate, would have nobly depicted him; would have dwelt with fondness upon his excellent qualities and characteristics, and all that distinguished him, in an age by no means prodigal of heroic virtues or extraordinary qualities of mind and heart; and would have assigned him no mean position amidst that illustrious company. And, under the influence of whatever motives his cotemporaries may be induced to regard him, it needs no prophetic vision to anticipate the fiat of posterity.

But since he is now so far removed from the effects of human censure or applause, it becomes us to consider how the republic may best derive benefit from his lamented death. His life is ours. But his death may avail us even more than his life, if we receive it as an admonition of the providence of God. If we are indeed a Christian people, we will not believe that the Supreme Ruler of the universe, without whom "not a sparrow falleth to the ground," has taken away the head and hope of the nation, at its hour of extremest need, without the design to impress some forgotten lesson upon our hearts. If it tend to lead us to more entire dependence upon Him; to repress the narrow and unworthy passions which agitate us; to soften the bitterness of party strife; to subdue the rancor of public and private animosities; to induce us to yield our partial views to considerations of the general welfare; to control and conquer sectional differences; to enhance in our eyes the value of sacred institutions, and to bind us more closely to our common country; could such be the result, neither the glorious recollections of his life, nor the sad memorials of his untimely death will have proved altogether in vain. And he, could he live to-day, would count his valued life but a willing sacrifice, to secure such blessings to the land he so loved and served.

And, with this imperfect tribute to the memory of a great and good man, I respectfully move that this Circuit Court of the United States do now adjourn.

LIFE AND WORKS OF FISHER AMES.*

[From the Monthly Law Reporter.]

THE written lives of great men are truly invaluable. If fairly and properly presented, there is no class of writing so useful, and it certainly loses nothing in this respect, by being usually entertaining as well as instructive. And we suppose, that nothing tends so much to keep up society, and to check that downward tendency, to which, by the law of nature, all human things are subject, as the example and instruction afforded by biographies of the illustrious departed. We are the more disposed to offer this consideration to the attention of our readers, because in our day a great deal has been said in derogation of what some have denominated "hero-worship;" especially by those who are willing to forget that the elements of great character, after all, must be great qualities; and who can, necessarily, offer us, as a substitute, only qualities, scarcely to be accounted so

* Works of Fisher Ames. With a Selection from his Speeches and Correspondence. Edited by his Son, Seth Ames. Boston: Little, Brown & Company. 1854.

well worthy of our respect and admiration. We acknowledge, for our own part, that we prefer to worship heroes, if need be, rather than those who have no title to any such appellation.

The reasons which go to constitute the sound basis, upon which our views in regard to this subject are founded, seem to us almost too obvious to require much effort at elucidation. The framework of human society, as we have already suggested, is not kept moving in regular order, and subject to just influences, by the mere operation of its own friction. On the contrary, if human affairs were left entirely to the management of those who, unhappily, possess no heroic tendencies, we apprehend that their ordinary pursuits would descend very low, in the scale of dignity and honor and whatever else tends to promote the improvement and elevation of the race. In a word, it is really great men, and not petty men,—men of noble minds and generous sympathies and elevated views and exalted talents,—those whose impulses and principles and aspirations conduct them honorably along the high and difficult paths of public service,—who undoubtedly deserve, as they have generally enjoyed, the peculiar respect and gratitude of mankind.

It sometimes happens, however, in the decay of States, under popular institutions, that men of no great ability or honor get the upper hand. In the midst of public factions and the jealousies and rivalries of political conflicts, hordes of the least deserving often become ambitious. The presumption of such persons is usually on a par with their ignorance, and they are unscrupulous, just in proportion as they are deficient in the higher sentiments, which control the conduct of better men. They are thus able, by means of combination and the impulse of common though selfish interest, to carry their objects into effect, and to exclude from the conduct of affairs those who are most able to understand and to manage them the best. The consequence always has been, and always will be, that a flood of degeneracy will sweep over the surface of society; and, unless checked by better influences, a nation, once enlightened, cultivated, generous and free, may become in the progress of time, as has often proved to be the case, degraded into barbarism, or its people supple slaves to the worst and meanest tyrants.

In a word, if free institutions are to flourish and be at all permanent, they must rest upon established principles of generally understood application, rather than stand openly exposed to the fluctuations of popular impulse or caprice; and the people who enjoy their advantages must vigilantly require, that the popular will shall be intelligently directed and expressed, and the laws be devised and administered by the ablest and best citizens, fitted to represent worthily the interests of the whole.

This, we observe, is an imperfect summary of Mr. Ames's political principles and opinions, for which some people saw fit, in his day, to stigmatize him as an aristocrat. In this view, and for the example and warning of other times, we conceive that his son has now conferred a real benefit on the public, by preparing this memorial of his illustrious father. For FISHER AMES was, unquestionably, a great man; of the true, old-fashioned, sterling, devoted stamp. Not, certainly, that we mean to be understood as alleging, that either he, or his cotemporaries, were quite free from errors and defects, which, in his case, it might be difficult to point out, but with which public men, in all ages and countries, have been more or less chargeable. Of one thing we are sorry to feel a clear confidence, that the standard of public obligation and the tone of public honor were altogether higher in his day than in our own; that the scale of generous patriotism had not generally been permitted a descent so low, and at the same time so safe, as more modern times have witnessed; and that political corruption as yet duly paid its decent and respectful external homage to public integrity. In a word, no one ever doubted, that we ever heard of, that Fisher Ames was an honest man; true to his principles, his conscience, his country and his Maker!

Throughout the great administration of Washington, during a period which, as Mr. Ames himself has admirably characterized it, "that government was administered with such integrity, without mystery, and in so prosperous a course, that it seemed wholly employed in acts of beneficence,"—and in subsequent more stormy times, side by side with men of powerful character and exalted ability, whose energies had been developed and concentrated, and vivified, amidst the stirring events of the revolution,—Mr. Ames was always seen in the front rank, and there he was seen, to the last, without a stain. We once heard one of his cotemporaries,* who knew him well, say, "Every body loved him." What a character is this! Better than fame, and more to be desired than the proudest rewards of all human ambition. To have passed through the troubled scenes of an eventful life, and the fierce, rancorous, unsparing conflicts of political warfare, with the general good-will, affords surely the highest testimonial, not merely of the excellent kindness of his heart, but of the sincere, unflinching and unsuspected uprightness of his character and life.

This is clearly no place, in which to indulge in speculations upon the principles of the great party, which he so long aided to conduct, with an ability, kindred, at least, to the highest genius, and a sagacity often prophetic, from the directness and singleness of

* The late Hon. I. P. Davis.

purpose with which he regarded public affairs. But the nature of these doctrines, in their general scope, and often in their minute details, and the earnest sincerity, which signalized his devotion to their elucidation and support, are sufficiently developed in the pages of these volumes.

We have styled Mr. Ames *illustrious*, and his titles to be thus distinguished we believe will be more fully acknowledged, the more closely they are investigated. They are, it is certain, of that solid character, which will bear the substantial test of time. The too narrow space, which our own pages allow us to afford to the notice of these handsome volumes, is due to the character of Mr. Ames, as an ornament to the profession of the Law; though the exigencies of the times, as well as his own inclinations, unquestionably, enlarged him into a statesman, instead of permitting the devotion of his life to the drudgery, or even to the higher pursuits of the Bar.

The volumes are introduced by that elegant and feeling sketch of Mr. Ames's life, prepared by the late President Kirkland, which has long been held one of the noblest tributes ever paid by one good man to the memory of another. This is followed by the "Letters," invaluable, of course, as sources of illustration of the public and private history of the times; and the second volume is made up of the political speeches and political essays of Mr. Ames. It is not our province to pronounce upon writings and oratorical efforts, which have, long since, taken their place in the public estimation. The Letters, now collected and published for the first time, constitute a new element of interest, and entitle the editor to our gratitude, for this highly valuable portion of his filial work. Our own publication is so exclusively devoted to the exposition of legal principles and the annals of judicial tribunals, that we are unable to devote any space to the consideration of the life and public character of Mr. Ames. This is the less necessary, however, by reason of the existence of that succinct and delightful personal sketch, by Dr. Kirkland, already alluded to.

The letters of Mr. Ames, however, we wish to remark, are of very great value. They run through the long period from 1789 to 1807 ; including, therefore, a series of years filled with events of the highest consequence, both to this country and to Europe, and covering that tract of time, in which the principles of our own government were most thoroughly examined, settled and established. They are written mostly offhand, in an easy, agreeable style, without any apparent deliberate attempt at artificial construction. Indeed, they are all addressed to his familiar friends, who were all men of mark in their day and generation. It constitutes their charm very much, therefore, as well as their value, that personal allusions, often to those of whose private life we cannot hear too much, and that suggestions in regard to domestic matters, of which more than we could wish appear to have been omitted, —are interspersed with discussions of public affairs, discriminating touches upon the motives and characters of public men, comments upon the temper and spirit of the people, forebodings, sometimes too soon realized, and ardent hopes and aspirations for the welfare of his country, generally far more than fulfilled. They present Mr. Ames in an aspect so attractive, through all the relations of life, as fairly to challenge credence to the remark of our venerable and now lamented friend, that "every body loved him." The body of one of these letters we quote below. It is, it will be seen, upon subjects kindred to our own pages. It throws some light upon the character of Mr. Ames, as a lawyer, and presents, in a striking view, his strong and sagacious sense,—indeed, it is actually prophetic in its judgments upon his cotemporaries,— and, in all respects, may be of service to members of the profession, in our own day. It is dated at Dedham, Mr. Ames's residence, October 5, 1802, and is addressed to Christopher Gore, afterwards Governor of Massachusetts, as we suppose on the eve of his return, from his embassy at London, to his native city, Boston. We would suggest, that a few more notes to these letters might be of use, and would save the trouble to their readers of tiresome research into cotemporary documents.

"You ask my advice about resuming the law business. I cheerfully undertake the office, only premising that in deciding the most momentous concerns of life, a man is not only his best, but almost solely, his own adviser. He has exclusively that instinctive perception of what he prefers, and of what he can do, that the most discerning friend must only suppose, and may, and indeed must, in a great measure mistake. Nevertheless, friends ought to advise, because they bring this power of *self*-judging into operation *precisely*, and with ample materials. All I will pretend to do is to frame a special verdict, and then humbly submit it to your honor's judgment.

"Great law knowledge is sure to gain business and emolument. The splendid eloquence that displays its treasures may hasten the popular judgment to decide that a man possesses them, but ultimately the learning of the lawyer decides the measure of his fame. Now, I pronounce that you are well fitted by nature and study, as well as practice, for such eminence, and by a practice that evinces your extensive learning and sound judgment as a lawyer, I cannot conceive that you will submit to an unfavorable test of character, or that you will be degraded from the place your friends wish to see you take.

"I will therefore assume it as a point proved, that by practice in great causes, and where law learning will be chiefly sought for, you will not impair the dignity of your standing by resorting to the bar. But you will reply, that by returning to open shop you cannot choose your customers, nor refuse to sell ordinary wares; to harangue a jury about the flogging given to a sailor, or to mingle in the snipsnap war about admitting a witness or a deposition, will often vex and humble the liberal mind; business of small value will not lie in your way. I reply, your share will be made up by insurance cases, and questions which our bankrupt law is sowing for the harvest of 1804. I observe that the little contests and litigations are engrossed by the junior class of the profession and by those who never advance beyond mediocrity. This is, I think, a different position of things from what existed in

1786. You will not calculate on the small fees, nor the vexatious litigation which concern sixpenny interests and sixpenny passions. Mr. Parsons practises on this large scale that I recommend; and I will add, fees are infinitely better than they were in 1786.

"Who are the rivals for this business with whom you must divide the booty? Parsons stands first, but he is growing older, less industrious, and wealth, or the hypo, may stop his practice. Otis is eager in the chase of fame and wealth, and, with a great deal of eloquence, is really a good lawyer, and improving. He, however, sighs for political office—he knows not what; and he will file off the moment an opportunity offers.

"Dexter is very able, and will be an Ajax at the bar as long as he stays. You know, however, that his aversion to reading and to practice are avowed, and I believe sincere. His head aches on reading a few hours, and if he did not love money very well, he would not pursue the law. Sullivan, who seems immortal, is admonished of his decay by a fit every three months, and will not be in your way.

"I, your humble servant, never was qualified by nature or inclination for the bar, and this I always well knew. Want of health, and the possession of a small competence will stop my mouth, if fate should not stop my breath before your return. I have reckoned all the persons who pretend to be considerable. John Lowell's health is wretched. . . . A number of eminent lawyers will be wanted in Boston, and though the place is overstocked, I think the prospect for 1804 not unhopeful. I know of no very dashing young men coming forward.

"Yet truth requires that I should, after all, state my expectation, that your share of the business will not be as great as it would have been if you had not left the country. It takes time to form connections and to resume the old set of clients. You are no chicken, and ought not to calculate on a very long period of drudgery at the bar. You will, and you ought to, enjoy the *otium cum amicis et libris et dignitate*, for many years before you die. I will not conceal from you my opinion, that you ought not to expect, or to take into your plan, the receipt of a great many great bags of money from your practice. I do not found this moderate calculation on your want of merit and talent, or on the refusal of the public to admit your title to both; I only insist that, from circumstances connected with you, with rivals in practice, and with the state of business, you are not to look for a very large income.

"Suppose, however, instead of six, eight or ten thousand dollars a year, which Hamilton and some others are said to derive from practice, you get only fifteen hundred or two thousand dollars, ought you to decline practice on that account, or to feel mortified, as if the public had rejected and degraded you? I am interested to insist that this estimate of reputation is not fair, for I am not entitled to boast of a lucrative practice. The truth is, other considerations deserve weight, and the public will give it to them.

"To be engaged on great law points, and to acquit yourself as you will, surely cannot fail to vindicate you with every body. Your time of life, your reputation, property, and moderation as to the passion for gain, will be assigned as reasons, even before you can assign them yourself, for your declining the toil of promiscuous business. It will be said, you would not be idle, nor will you be a drudge. This line of practice, the only one in your choice, will shelter you from the ungentlemanly wrangles of the bar, and the courts have of late years set about learning some manners.

"Then the question is fairly before you, whether you will open your shop on such terms, and with such prospects as I have stated. Why not? I ask. You will, or some friends rather of yours will reply, why should Mr. Gore descend to this not very respectable, not very comfortable, not very lucrative fagging at the bar? I urge that it is better to keep up your style of living by some business, than to change it for an idle life, and a style observably lower than that you have been accustomed to. A man may make some retrenchments and savings, but he cannot greatly alter his expense without *descending*, which I should be sorry you should have forced upon you. A man may not incline to take a certain degree on the scale of genteel living, but having once taken it he must maintain it. Still I think that law in Boston will keep you out of the way of spending fifteen hundred or two thousand dollars, that a retirement of idle luxury would impose upon you at Waltham. Every southern visitor must see your improvements, show them to his wife, and eat and drink you ten guineas' worth. $2000 saved, and $2000 got, is $4000, enough to meet all the demands on your treasury, over and above the resources drawn from your property. Perhaps the superior cheapness of living in Boston may not strike you. I reply, a busy man may make savings and reputably, if he will; and indeed he must renounce business, or be moderate in his pleasures. He must often draw a special plea and refuse a feast. This is not all. Make the comparison between business and no business. Farming at Waltham will be some resource, but I have no idea that it will afford that steady occupation which is essential to keep life from being a heavy burden. Books, you will say, afford that resource. In some degree they do, but they need auxiliary resources. In case you should be at Waltham, unemployed by the public, you will be in some danger of being forgotten by the great multitude—out of sight out of mind, is their maxim. By practice you will be in sight, and ready, in every one's mind, for such public employment as your friends will say ought to seek you. Therefore the bar is in my judgment the best place for you to occupy, whether you aim at economy in expense, tranquil enjoyment of friends, or the resumption of any public station. Your social affections will find objects and exercise; you will be kept busy, and of course cheerful; you will not appear to be laid by or thrown away, but to have chosen your old post. Even if you should do little business, the extent of your sacrifice will be the more apparent. You will return, not with a raging thirst of gain, but with a resolution to study your cases and to merit confidence and reputation.

"Hence I conclude you ought to 'open shop' again. On conversing with Mr. Cabot, I confess he instantly decided the point against me; on further discussion he came over to my opinion. Indeed, it seems to me not merely the best course, but the only one left to you. All which is humbly submitted.

FISHER AMES, *Foreman*."—p. 299.

This letter, thus playfully framed and subscribed, affords us a fair specimen of Mr. Ames's epistolary style. It exhibits also, in a remarkable degree, that extraordinary good sense, which, applied to affairs of more general interest, is denominated wisdom; implying a grasp of mind and soundness of judgment and a faculty of sagacious discrimination, which are the rarest of human gifts. With this no one can doubt Mr. Ames was eminently endowed. He has been sometimes styled "the Burke of America." Such comparisons often fail in some essential particulars; and in the present instance, we suppose would be understood as intimating some inferiority to his great prototype, on the part of the American statesman. In our opinion, not rashly formed, Mr. Ames, with a cast of mind and genius and a nervous organization, in some respects essentially similar to the characteristics of Mr. Burke, may well be held fully the equal of that great man, except on the score of general learning; for the acquisition and cultivation of which, this country afforded fewer opportunities and inducements than, at that time at least, existed abroad. He was, nevertheless, an elegant scholar, as we gather from the memoir, already adverted to; a fact, indeed, sufficiently apparent not merely from the classical allusions to be found in his speeches, letters and political essays; but from that ardor and glow and elevation of thought, which show clearly that his mind had been at those great sources of inspiration, whose draughts invigorate and ennoble minds of any kindred warmth. The grand essays of Mr. Burke, rich in all the resources of his luxuriant and subtle imagination, were in reality addressed to the higher mind of society; that is, to that audience of cultivated and educated people, whose minds were capable of becoming imbued with the spirit of his powerful and generous, but frequently abstract speculations; and whose influence upon the administration of public affairs might be, therefore, rather reflective than direct. The briefer pieces of Mr. Ames, employing, generally and from necessity, no higher vehicle of communication with the public, than the newspapers of the day, were far more practical concessions to such claims, as the people themselves might be thought to have upon his instruction and advice. Yet they are dignified and enhanced by the weight of his learning, and glow with the illuminating fire of his genius. We should be disposed to indicate, as one chief point of difference, that Mr. Burke *thought*, while Mr. Ames both *thought and felt*. We do not mean to be understood, that in our opinion the great British statesman, for whom we claim to entertain an unsurpassed admiration, was really deficient in true manly feeling; but that the emotions caught from the imagination, in the closet, must be necessarily somewhat colder than the spontaneous and natural bursts of the heart.

In one important particular, our own countryman must bear away the palm. No man surpassed him in his faculty of engrossing the profound attention and regard of his audience, and few speeches have so thoroughly won the great object of speeches by results, so immediately triumphant and overwhelming, as his own. Indeed, the clear logical deductions, the soul of imagination, the depth of earnest feeling, the statesmanlike knowledge, the philosophical analysis, the force of reasoning, the power, aptness and elegance of expression,—all combined in his great speech on the British Treaty, delivered in the House of Representatives of the United States, April 28, 1796,—are so animated by the vigor, and, so to speak, elastic spring of the style, that we who read can have no hesitation as to its influence on those who heard it. It was of this speech that John Quincy Adams,—certainly no incompetent judge,—who had listened, under very favorable circumstances, to all the distinguished orators of the British Parliament, at its most brilliant period,—to Burke, and Pitt, and Sheridan, and Fox,—and who had heard and observed all that our own Congress could produce, when the great men of those times led on the contending parties,—pronounced, "There could be no doubt of it—of all that he had ever heard—Mr. Ames's speech on the British Treaty was surely the most eloquent."

The closing paragraphs of this noble appeal to the

honor, as well as the judgment and reason of the nation, which afford, however, a very inadequate idea of its general character, are exceedingly touching and beautiful. If it be literally true, as we have no question it was substantially so, that this speech was delivered without any of that mature antecedent reflection, and direct, careful preparation, with which most of the grandest efforts of the human mind have been wrought out, we should scarcely know where to look for its parallel.

"Let me cheer the mind, weary no doubt, and ready to despond on this prospect, by presenting another, which it is yet in our power to realize. Is it possible for a real American to look at the prosperity of this country, without some desire for its continuance, without some respect for the measures which, many will say produced, and all will confess have preserved, it? Will he not feel some dread, that a change of system will reverse the scene? The well-grounded fears of our citizens, in 1794, were removed by the treaty, but are not forgotten. Then they deemed war nearly inevitable, and would not this adjustment have been considered at that day as a happy escape from the calamity? The great interest and the general desire of our people was to enjoy the advantages of neutrality. This instrument, however misrepresented, affords America that inestimable security. The causes of our disputes are either cut up by the roots, or referred to a new negotiation, after the end of the European war. This was gaining everything, because it confirmed our neutrality, by which our citizens are gaining everything. This alone would justify the engagements of the government. For, when the fiery vapors of the war lowered in the skirts of our horizon, all our wishes were centered in this one, that we might escape the desolation of the storm. This treaty, like a rainbow on the edge of the cloud, marked to our eyes the space where it was raging, and afforded at the same time the sure prognostic of fair weather. If we reject it, the vivid colors will grow pale; it will be a baleful meteor portending tempest and war.

"Let us not hesitate, then, to agree to the appropriation to carry it into faithful execution. Thus we shall save the faith of our nation, secure its peace, and diffuse the spirit of confidence and enterprise that will augment its prosperity. The progress of wealth and improvement is wonderful, and some will think, too rapid. The field for exertion is fruitful and vast, and if peace and good government should be preserved, the acquisitions of our citizens are not so pleasing as the proofs of their industry, as the instruments of their future success. The rewards of exertion go to augment its power. Profit is every hour becoming capital. The vast crop of our neutrality is all seed-wheat, and is sown again, to swell, almost beyond calculation, the future harvest of prosperity. In this progress what seems to be fiction is found to fall short of experience.

"I rose to speak under impressions that I would have resisted if I could. Those who see me will believe, that the reduced state of my health has unfitted me, almost equally, for much exertion of body or mind. Unprepared for debate by careful reflection in my retirement, or by long attention here, I thought the resolution I had taken, to sit silent, was imposed by necessity, and would cost me no effort to maintain. With a mind thus vacant of ideas, and sinking, as I really am, under a sense of weakness, I imagined the very desire of speaking was extinguished by the persuasion that I had nothing to say. Yet when I come to the moment of deciding the vote, I start back with dread from the edge of the pit into which we are plunging. In my view even the minutes I have spent in expostulation have their value, because they protract the crisis, and the short period in which alone we may resolve to escape it.

"I have thus been led by my feelings to speak more at length than I had intended. Yet I have perhaps as little personal interest in the event as any one here. There is, I believe, no member who will not think his chance to be a witness of the consequences greater than mine. If, however, the vote should pass to reject, and a spirit should rise, as it will, with the public disorders, to make 'confusion worse confounded,' even I, slender and almost broken as my hold upon life is, may outlive the government and constitution of my country."—p. 69.

Fisher Ames was born at Dedham, Massachusetts, April 9, 1758. There he continued to live, except as public duties required his presence at the seat of government. "His spotless youth," says Dr. Kirkland, "brought blessings to the whole remainder of his life." At his native place he died July 4, 1808; a day fitly closing, though too early, the valuable life of a true patriot, in peace and honor. There was a great deal in his mind, manners, habits, and general character, which might well have commended his memory to the old Greek biographer. His last thoughts dwelt deeply upon his country, and upon a condition of public affairs, which he had employed his best talents and energies all his life long to avert. He regarded the doctrines, upon which the national administration was then conducted, with a feeling akin to horror. The same venerable friend whom we have before mentioned, and who related this incident to the author while he was preparing this article, visited him, in company with Mr. Cabot, about ten days before his departure. He was then in bed. The conversation fell upon the disheartening aspect of the times and the dangers threatening the public safety, from the discordant elements then at work. "The Union must be preserved," said Mr. Ames; "things are bad enough; but anything is better than dissolution."

HON. CHARLES JACKSON.

[From the Monthly Law Reporter.]

We have already announced, as it occurred, the lamented decease of this eminent jurist and citizen. Our number for January, 1856, contained some brief account of the proceedings of the Suffolk bar, in recognition of the event; of the presentation of becoming resolutions to the Supreme Court of the State, and of the appropriate response of Chief Justice Shaw. The scene in the court-room, which place is usually supposed to be little better than a mere arena for the combats of trained and conflicting intellects, was, upon this occasion, peculiarly affecting. The hall itself was thronged with a dense assembly of the legal brethren and personal friends of the great lawyer departed, and of others, whom various motives of curiosity or interested feeling draw together upon like occasions. It was a happy circumstance, that one of the late judge's former pupils, himself a well-known leader at the bar, offered, and, we presume, prepared, the resolutions agreed upon, as the expression of the common sentiment. They thus derived, from the influence of familiar intercourse and the ardor of private friendship, combined with long habits of well-founded respect for the character of the deceased, a point, a scope, a fitness, and a genial glow of sympathy, correspondent with the requirements of the subject and the occasion, and far surpassing the ordinary formal tone of many similar ceremonials. And whoever had the fortune to listen to the reply of the venerable Chief Justice, often interrupted by the intensity of his feelings, must have perceived, that neither the wear and tear of the most extensive professional practice, commonly reckoned a somewhat hardening, as well as hard, school of experience,—nor the loftier demands of eminent judicial position, necessarily chill the natural flow of human emotion, or make or leave a truly great lawyer anything other than the true man, which nature intended him to be.

It was observable here, however, as must almost always be the case, that the statement of the deliberate judgment of those who took part in the proceedings, so far as the character of the mere lawyer was concerned, comprehended only certain terms of generalization, highly honorable and laudatory it is true, although not especially distinctive,—but equally applicable to many who have gone before, as they will be to others who may come up hereafter. This is the fortune, we will not call it the misfortune, of the profession. It is the fate of the great leader at the bar, to make but a temporary mark and to be summarily forgotten. His life may be one of extraordinary activity and bustle. He may seem to live in the full blaze of the world's admiring eye. He may be engaged, through a protracted series of years, in the management of successive causes, which demand the exertion of all his energies and faculties, and often, perhaps, enlist all his feelings, and which may involve the very highest human responsibilities; and, within a very few years after he has passed off the stage, his very name will have become obliterated from the memory of men, or be only occasionally recalled, within the compass of a very limited circle.

The poet, with somewhat less than his usual observance of exact justice, supposes Fame to be niggardly enough to resume her awards of honor, even those bestowed upon her chiefest favorites, if a single misfortune should occur to mar the chain of successful achievements:

> "The painful warrior famoused for fight,
> After a thousand victories, once foiled,
> Is from the book of honor razed quite,
> And all the rest forgot, for which he toiled."

But the great lawyer, in this country, who has advanced through successive triumphs, to the very pinnacle of professional reputation, may hope in vain to erect any lasting monument to his memory, unless, indeed, his abilities, usually at the hazard of his legal standing, and assuredly to his pecuniary loss, have found a field of exercise in the senate as well as the forum; or, unless he be willing to sacrifice his professional emoluments, for the inadequate compensation which attends the honor of the bench, and thus secures, at least, a legal immortality, through his elaborate judgments recorded in the books. It is also true, that the tenor of mere professional life has been usually found to be too uneventful for biography. And undoubtedly the objects, upon which the most eminent advocate employs his faculties at the bar, are generally of very transient interest. His chief business, after all, is only to apply long-discovered and well-established principles to the varying conditions of human affairs. And, however absorbing may be his immediate sympathy with each individual case, the actual interest in the settlement of questions of abstract right is very much confined to the parties directly concerned. Even if the habits of his life permitted him to glance, with the eye of imagination, upon family secrets intrusted to him, sometimes far surpassing the ordinary boundaries of fiction, in passionate intensity of detail and in extraordinary development of character, or, if professional honor authorized him to make them known,—still, his own peculiar part, in the control or management of such incidents, is little more than that of the good fairy in Oriental tales, who appears at the proper moment certainly, to relieve virtuous distress or to defeat impending malice; but his own intervention is, after all, only incidental, and the main points of interest would, by no means, afford the appropriate materials for his own personal biography.

It sometimes happens, however, that the natural character of the man stands out so prominently and remarkably, outside of his professional, and, we may say, his adventitious position, that the general cause of human good is likely to be advanced, by selecting such an instance for our special observation and example. In the present instance, it affords us a melancholy satisfaction to devote some portion of our pages to such a brief memoir of the late Judge Jackson as our materials permit. For, in a peculiar sense, the event of his death, at an age very much exceeding the ordinary bounds of human existence, derived its importance from the tenor of his life; and we are unwilling that one, in whose character goodness was so fittingly conjoined with intellectual superiority, should pass entirely out of our sight, without some appropriate notice in our pages. He was born in Newburyport, May 31st, 1775, and died at his residence, Bedford Place, Boston, December 13, 1855. Having thus exceeded the great age of eighty years, he afforded a signal example of those, who prove to what an advanced period a feeble constitution may be made subservient and serviceable to the uses and control of the mind. Indeed, very many of his latter years had been spent in a manner so secluded from public observation, that few of the present generation would be likely to know what an important professional and judicial position he once occupied. As he occasionally appeared in the streets, however, accompanied by his attendant, no observant stranger could fail to indulge in some curious speculation upon the history of that feeble old man, with the pale and thoughtful face; and the universal respect of those who recognized him often must have excited a still deeper interest and prompted more earnest inquiry. He was, indeed, one of the few remaining links of that chain, fast loosening its hold, and very soon to be drawn back into the irrevocable past, which connects our times with a period, one day to be looked upon as the great and heroic age of this country; a period not of perfect men certainly, but of a large and influential class of those, who were bolder and nobler, as it seems to us, and more disinterestedly brave and self-sacrificing in the public service, than is common now,—of men who were eminent above the measure of this day in the various pursuits of professional life,—and were gentlemen in the ordinary intercourse of society, by the example, the cultivation and the public recognition of honor, integrity, and just and generous sentiment.

So far as these causes might tend to the formation of a worthy and admirable character, Judge Jackson had the advantage of them in the circle of his early acquaintance, and especially in the home of his youth. For his father was truly a prince amongst merchant princes,—an ardent patriot, a thorough Washingtonian in politics, a Federalist of the old school,—what would now probably be called an aristocrat, unless he may be considered to have somewhat qualified this stigmatic appellation, by undeviating devotion to the cause of the country, by the most generous efforts and sacrifices in its behalf, by the faithful performance of every private duty, and the clear and able discharge of many high public trusts; in fact, by entire integrity and purity of life, and unsurpassed courtesy of manners; securing to himself universal respect while he lived, and the common lamentation when he died, and enabling him to leave to his children a name better than rubies, and which had its undoubted influence in the formation of their characters, and in the tenor of their histories and fortunes.

At the period of Judge Jackson's birth, Newburyport, the place of his father's origin and residence then, and long afterwards, and during his most prosperous days, stood amongst the first, if it was not the highest, on the list of the secondary class of towns on the American coast. It still retains its natural beauty, its ancient mansions, and much else which yet constitutes it a place of no common interest. But many of the elements of its former distinction have long since passed away. In those days, however, it was to this town that young men were often sent from the capital, and elsewhere, to learn the skill, the habits, the discipline and the principles then deemed requisite for a merchant; for there were the counting-rooms of men who, besides the evidence of their successful enterprise, had secured the public confidence, by eminent services performed and marked ability displayed in the public cause. Jonathan Jackson, the father of the judge, was a man of education and accomplishment, as well as talent, and was a valuable member of the Continental Congress in the year 1780. His townsman, Tristram Dalton, equally eminent as a merchant and a man, was one of the two senators first elected to Congress by Massachusetts under the constitution; and Nathaniel Tracy, uncle of Judge Jackson, more successful than either, in the acquisitions of maritime enterprise, is reputed to have supplied government with no less than one hundred and sixty-seven thousand dollars, during the revolutionary war—out of a fortune so ample, as to make the question of repayment of such a sum a matter of indifference, and which was really sacrificed by a private gentleman to the general necessity. Men like these, with their compeers, of more or less pretension and success, would naturally give a very decided character to a town; and many agreeable associations, which make its name more than usually familiar, are to be traced back to this day of its former pride and prosperity.

At the same period, also, Newburyport was the residence of Chief Justice Theophilus Parsons, then in the zenith of his preëminent professional reputation,—from whose office Rufus King, John Quincy Adams, Robert Treat Paine, Benjamin Gorham, and a long file of other distinguished persons,—of whom, we believe one, Mr. Charles Phelps of Hadley, still survives,—entered upon their various useful and brilliant courses of life. There, also, resided the bishop of the diocese of Massachusetts, Dr. Bass, and Dr. Spring, father of Gardiner Spring of New York, and who had been chaplain to Arnold's romantic expedition for the conquest of Quebec, which took its departure from Newburyport, and who was, afterwards, a chaplain in the regular army; and there was Murray, the Presbyterian minister, than whom no more eloquent, or more learned divine of the times could be named,—and there, Whitfield, the wonder of his day, who, for many years, had occasionally preached to the inhabitants, had died, not long before, and found that rest, which its earth still affords to his bones. There was also the early instructor of Charles Jackson, Nicholas Pike, author of the first American arithmetic, of whom one of his biographers says—

"He was ready in the classics, and seldom took a book to hear his pupils recite,"—and close by, at Dummer Academy, was "Master Moody," famous above all others, and preceptor of many of the leading men of the last century. It was the home, also, of the excellent and beloved physician of this distinguished circle, and of the poor quite as much, Dr. Swett, father of Col. Samuel Swett of this city—and whose name, after the lapse of sixty years from his decease, still

Smells sweet and blossoms in the dust,—

though a physician not often has the opportunity, or the fortune, to leave behind him much enduring memorial of his fame. There, also, was Judge Bradbury, of the Supreme Court, with whom Parsons studied, and Dudley Atkins Tyng, collector of the port under Washington, and afterwards reporter of the early volumes of the Massachusetts decisions, and connected with some of the principal families of Massachusetts; and there were born, a few years before, John Lowell, son of the famous Judge John Lowell, and in the same year with Charles Jackson, Francis C. Lowell, brother of John, to whom our chief manufacturing city owes its origin and its name. Here, also, might be found, during the youth of Jackson, a very considerable body of revolutionary worthies, amongst them a general officer, distinguished at

Bunker-hill, and others who attained high rank in the military service of the country, in the course of the war. No town upon our seaboard entered into that long struggle, with readier or higher spirit than Newburyport; and it is easy to conceive how the character of its veteran sons, returning from the triumphant issue of so great a cause, must have tended to promote its general elevation and respectability. Under such circumstances, therefore, and amidst such influences, the subject of this notice was born and bred, while there existed in his place of birth an energy, an elevation, a style of living, a tone of society and a spirit, scarcely to be imagined in one of the lesser seaport towns of our own time. We fear that we may have been betrayed into a too fond recital of departed glories and worthies; but it is not, we believe, without its use, and we rejoice that there are those yet left, to whom it will prove a subject of unfailing interest.

We have no intention of writing any elaborate sketch of the life of Judge Jackson, even were we qualified for this duty, by anything more than an ordinary familiarity with the distinguishing traits of his character. Our only hope has been, to be able to pay some not unfitting tribute to the memory of a good citizen, and a good man.

After spending the period of his youth in his native town, he entered Cambridge college, at an early age, in the same class with the late Dr. Pierce of Brookline, and Charles Coffin of his own town, afterwards president of Greenville and Knoxville colleges, in Tennessee, and who was his nearest competitor for the highest college honors, which Jackson secured. He pursued the study of the law with Parsons, at Newburyport; and it was either in regard to the period of his legal studies, or to that immediately after he entered upon the practice of his profession, of which we have heard it said, in his own town, that *he never looked at a newspaper for three years.* Such an instance of self-restraint, in a young man, and of devotion to his peculiar duties, certainly gave evidence of qualities, significant of his future eminence in a profession, which he had thus made the sole mistress of his affections. Accordingly, he won the entire approbation of a teacher not easy to please, and Parsons is known to have said of him, when he entered upon practice—"Of all my pupils, no one has left my office better fitted for his profession"—[and it is to be remembered that King and Adams had preceded him]—"he will prove himself the American Blackstone." No man could be better qualified than Parsons to form an accurate judgment on such a subject, and we have no doubt the prediction was fully warranted by the elegance, the extent, and the soundness of his pupil's acquisitions. If it eventually failed in its specific application, the cause of such deficiency is to be assigned to enfeebled health, rather than to any want of the necessary ability and accomplishment. But, notwithstanding his devotion to his profession, Mr. Jackson was said to be the most popular young man in Newburyport; a distinction owing, no doubt, to the excellence of his disposition, to that amenity of manners, which was in him a peculiarly observable trait, and to the unspotted purity of his life,—as well as to a natural pride in the ability and character of a young townsman,—for which laudable and patriotic feeling, the citizens of his native town have often shown a remarkable predisposition.

With such qualities and advantages, it must follow, as a matter of course, that Mr. Jackson would rise, steadily and rapidly, to the highest position of professional eminence. At the bar, he was trusted, beloved and honored; and when, eventually, he received the appointment of one of the justices of the Supreme Court of the State, upon the decease of Judge Sedgwick, in the year 1813, it was with the approbation of all good men. We have always been informed that Judge Jackson was what might be styled a *model judge;* that he was distinguished upon the bench, which he adorned for only the brief period of about ten years, for a marked composure of demeanor, for entire precision of legal learning, for extraordinary urbanity of manner, for an absolute freedom from passion or prejudice, for a certain, native, high-minded independence of opinion, and for an impartiality, which amounted, as nearly as possible, to the exemplification of abstract justice; yet, with a decisive inclination, whenever the opportunity occurred, to present the equitable view of a case. We need not say, therefore, that he exhibited that first qualification of a judge—uprightness—a characteristic, happily, of judicial position in Massachusetts, as a general rule, and maintaining itself comparatively unsullied, even to our own somewhat wavering times. But we firmly believe, if the memory of any one of those who have passed off the stage, in the bright array of Massachusetts judges, were to be appealed to, for a signal example of judicial purity, the name of Charles Jackson would be the first to occur. And, since the position of a judge upon the earth is not, as it is too often considered, that of a mere man of business, according to the ordinary estimate of human affairs, but he is, in some imperfect sense, the vice-chancellor and substitute of infinite wisdom, justice, and power, —we know not what more could be said in honor of any person, or why any one could wish to bequeath a clearer and nobler reputation to his country.

There are certain opinions of Judge Jackson, in the books, which may be referred to as leading and most valuable judgments. But any special detail of their merits would be out of place here. In consequence of failing health, he resigned his office in 1823, and the public thus lost the benefit of those services, which he might, perhaps, have rendered during some considerable portion, at least, of the subsequent thirty years granted to his honored life. For the purpose of relaxation and recovery, he soon sailed for England; and as evidence of a reputation not confined to home or native country, and of personal characteristics well fitted to promote his intercourse with intelligent and cultivated society everywhere, we quote from a letter of a gentleman, writing from London to a friend in Newburyport:—"Two of your townsmen" (the other was Jacob Perkins) "now fill the public eye of England, and are the subjects of public and private conversation."

The remaining years of Judge Jackson's life were passed in studious retirement, and in agreeable communion with an extended circle of family and social friends. In 1836 he was appointed head of the commission, under the resolve of the legislature, for the revision of the statutes of Massachusetts, of the character of which important undertaking we need say nothing. Excepting this arduous labor, and the publication of his learned treatise on Real Actions, to be referred to an earlier date, we are aware of no other public service performed by him, while he was, indeed, necessarily and carefully nursing the often flickering flame of life. In politics, he clung with the ardor and tenacity of settled principle to the ancient faith of the old Essex platform, of which his master, Parsons, so admirably sketched the outline in his famous "Resolutions;" upon the basis of which so many of the noblest men, whom this country has ever counted amongst its jewels, have so often uttered words of warning and wisdom and encouragement and patriotism, in the roughest times the country has ever seen. In religion, he was, as we have good reason to believe, what was said with equal truth of John Selden, "a resolved serious Christian;" and, unlike too many professional men, he found no excuse for the neglect of its duties, in the engrossing demands of ordinary cares and labors. Indeed, his life was one long routine of fulfilled duties, which a natural sense of rectitude made pleasures. We presume he had faults, for he was human; if so, they were not public, and we know not what they were. He was a gentleman, by nature, sentiment, and cultivation. During his whole life, he was beloved, esteemed and respected. He dies, without a blot upon his memory, and has thus nobly fulfilled the only real purposes of human existence.

MR. CHOATE'S LECTURE

ON

ROGERS AND HIS TIMES.

We imagine, it will be found not a very easy matter to present even an intelligible sketch of Mr. Choate's great lecture, delivered on Monday evening. No description could really furnish any adequate idea of such a performance. As well might mortal painter endeavor to catch upon canvas those hues of heaven, which kindle into beauty and vanish in the trail of the descending day. And just as no imagination could recall those shapes of capricious loveliness, momentarily shifting and finally melting into that unfathomable ocean of golden light; so those who have subsequently attempted to report this great orator (for assuredly no gray goose-quill, detached from its parent wing, could be quite fleet enough to follow him, at the moment) have thus found the vividness, the glow, the rapidity, and the sparkle of his utterly unexpected diagonalisms, quite beyond the reach of their ability to set down.

Whoever has been in the habit of hearing Mr. Choate at the bar, or upon occasions of public interest, could not fail to be prepared to listen to a discourse, instinct with thought, glittering with the fire of genius, bubbling and boiling over with the stir and riotous action of a teeming and irrepressible fancy. Confessedly, it is a very extraordinary thing, that this great, laborious, and eminently successful lawyer, who occupies a place at the Bar, with no man above, and no man very near him; who so wonderfully exemplifies the axiom, that the part is contained in the whole —as it is in complete and not in imperfect works—by employing constantly the minutest technical details of his profession, with the same unvarying, accurate skill, as that with which he grasps its broadest principles and wields the entire machinery of its philosophical learning; and who devotes more daily hours to the trial and argument of causes, than any three or four other persons together; that such a man, so gifted, so constituted, and so occupied, should have kept his mind thoroughly imbued with the freshness of earlier literary and classical acquisitions—should have pressed on breast-high with whatever is worthy of attention in the literature of to-day, and, on an occasion like the present, should have been able to charm, delight, and, we may say, fascinate an audience as intelligent and cultivated as, we presume, is ordinarily assembled in this or any other American city.

We doubt very much whether such an exhibition could be had anywhere else, or from any other source. Mr. Choate is a person eminently idiosyncratic. There is not, and never was, a speaker exactly like him; and we have never heard anybody speak who, by the gift of nature, knew better how to present his strong points in their most attractive aspect, or to make his weak ones tell more effectively. For the public performances of Mr. Choate, judged according to the strict canons of art, are by no means perfect. A cold criticism, subsequently applied, (for we suppose only a very cold critic would think of such a criterion, under the immediate spell of the orator's fascinating eloquence), may undoubtedly detect inequalities, deficiencies, thought too rapidly conceived, expressions now and then inadequately chosen. For our own part, we confess our disposition to yield ourselves up to the madness of the hour. So far from allowing ourselves to be diverted from the general effect of a noble performance, like that of Monday evening, by any of those occasional irregular but characteristic lapses, we should as soon think of quitting the broad bosom of the glorious river, which is floating us prosperously on towards happiness and home, for any of the side-creeks and false bays, into which the abounding stream pours some of its superfluous waters.

It would be equally unfair and useless to undertake to judge Mr. Choate by any of the ordinary standards.

In some sense, like Shakspeare's, his genius exceeds their bounds, and is not, therefore, amenable to their laws. His mind is full to overflowing; and the infinite relations of things, in their remoter as well as their more intimate coherences, present themselves to his imagination and are made subservient to his uses, in a manner not always easily to be appreciated by a common mind. We dare say there are those, in his own profession or out of it, in the same sphere of life, who no more understand him, in his loftier flights, than they do poetry, in the very ecstasy of its inspiration. We have seen persons to whom *Rachel* appeared absolutely ugly, or, at least, as exhibiting only the icy, outside glitter of a sort of fiendish fascination, in the manifestation of her extraordinary powers; to others she seemed almost divinely lovely, and the express personification of all those qualities and capacities, which occasionally prove how humanity may sometimes get wings and soar out of the dead level of mere passionless routine and mediocrity. This casual comparison is by no means a fanciful one; for there is a good deal of resemblance between these two remarkable personages, of different countries, callings, and sexes. In his public efforts, Mr. Choate unfolds, in no mean degree, those blended shades of pathos and humor, which betoken tragic power; and we have often thought, that on the stage he would have shown himself a tragic actor, as incomparable, as he is without a competitor at the Bar.

There will always be carpers at such characters. Through some perversity of nature, men seem often to take pleasure in bolstering up weakness and inanity, and in throwing obstacles in the way of whatever asserts genuine claims to superiority. Genius finally wins its way to its uppermost heights, only through clouds and storms; or to drop the figure, through envy and detraction, faint praise accorded, or in spite of assent altogether withheld. It would sometimes seem an almost inevitable rule, that men agree, with one consent, to praise that which needs it most, and to tear away, on the other hand, from great merit whatever fairly belongs to it. In the one case, no man's self-love is wounded, by commending that which he conceives to be somewhat beneath his own powers; in the other, every concession which he makes is only an acknowledgment of his own individual inferiority. Of course, a man like Mr. Choate is beyond all these impediments to his progress now, and can look down upon them compassionately, unless he prefers, as we hope, to look up. But we should like to see those, who are most inclined to disparage such a lecture as Mr. Choate delivered, try to imitate it, and so soon learn that, whether it seem to them great or small, in its height or breadth, its golden profusion, and its rolling, overflowing, flashing tide of thought and illustration, it would be found quite beyond the range of their most ambitious efforts, as much as some of its flights really transcend the capacity of ordinary conception. In fact, it requires much higher powers, to accomplish any great work, however subject to critical exception, than to discover and point out those inevitable imperfections, to which all human performances are liable.

We did not set out with any purpose of offering an analysis of this remarkable lecture. We have heard the observation, that it was not exactly what was to be expected of Mr. Choate—which, we suppose, means that it did not entirely correspond with certain indefinite and extravagant expectations, which no man ever did or ever can satisfy. We thought it quite equal to his best efforts, and if not, yet in certain respects superior to what other men could do. It exhibited all those points, which are sometimes accounted amongst the faults of this eminent orator, and it glittered with the fervor and showering fire of genius—flinging out a word, here and there, which sparkled in its place like some diamond of incomparable lustre—drawing its illustrations out of clefts and caverns at the height of the rocks, inaccessible to the sweep of ordinary thought, or from depths of the sea, which only the imagination of the hardiest diver would venture to explore.

We have also heard this performance characterized

as discursive. To our apprehension, it possessed a certain higher order and propriety of parts, sufficiently luminous in itself, and amply consistent with its subject. Other critics have suggested, we are told, that some of its channels of thought indicated the results of Mr. Choate's reading, amongst the great writers of our own and of other times. We have little doubt, without making any reference for the sake of comparison, that the beautiful tribute to old age, with which Mr. Choate ushered in his address, may have much coincidence of sentiment with that noblest essay of Cicero, "De Senectute." We should judge that Mr. Choate had been a reader of Lord Bacon. We make no question his mind has been more or less imbued with the vital sentiment of certain works, showing how a new style and spirit of modern letters sprang out of the embers of the French Revolution, like the young and vigorous growth covering with fresh luxuriance the ashes of the forest, swept over by consuming fire; it was quite evident he is an admirer of the fathers and leaders of English literature,—the ornaments, the honors, and lights of the world, upon whose writings the mind feeds and grows, and to which it is indebted for furnishing it with new thought, or recalling the old which had been forgotten.

He who has accustomed himself to habitual association with such writers no more loses his own individuality, than the flower forfeits its native form and beauty, though it developes a lovelier hue and grace, when it is transplanted into a more congenial soil. By consequence of such studies, instead of immature thought, crude and feeble conception and elaborate shallowness, or a mere vacant and meretriciously bedizened essay, like a hollow pillar of sapless wood, encircled with artificial flowers,—we have just such a fresh, thoughtful, suggestive, glowing lecture,—the more liable to be misappreciated, since it was certainly very far out of the common course,—as that with which Mr. Choate enchanted an expressively silent audience, for an hour and a half, on Monday evening. It was gratifying beyond measure to listen to those philosophical deductions of principles and results, so broad, sound, generous and noble, so fitted to advance truth, to maintain honor, to dignify manhood, to cheer and sweeten life. Even if we might not assent to all its critical exemplifications and instances, in our opinion the lecture was such a lofty and generous intellectual effort, that we wish we knew where to look, either now or for the future, in order to justify our hope of other such literary performances.

If we were to select, after that most happy and self-deprecatory opening, the portion of the lecture which seemed to us more than usually admirable, it was the reply to Carlyle's futile blow at Walter Scott. There could remain no doubt on the mind of whoever was present, that this splendid and carefully wrought passage went thrilling to the hearts of the assembly, and filled and satisfied their understandings with an argument at once eloquent, original, and conclusive. For our own part, we can only express our wish, that an intellectual exercise of such extraordinary power and brilliancy, and calculated to produce so salutary an influence, might be in the hands, as well as in the ears and mouths of the public; and we sincerely trust that Mr. Choate may be induced to yield his reluctance, for this once, and put forth in print a performance, which we cannot help feeling confident would tend very much to the benefit of his permanent reputation.

A SHAKESPEARIAN RESEARCH.

THAT passage of Shakespeare, which has given occasion to numerous annotations and disquisitions, perhaps the most unprofitably long drawn out, is the one quoted below. It occurs in that passionate monologue of Juliet, uttered while she is impatiently awaiting the approach of night, to cover her concerted interview with Romeo:—

> Gallop apace, you fiery-footed steeds,
> Towards Phœbus' mansion; such a wagoner
> As Phaeton would whip you to the West,
> And bring in cloudy night immediately;
> Spread thy close curtain, love-performing night!
> That *runaway's eyes may wink*, and Romeo
> Leap to these arms, untalked of and unseen, &c.
>
> ROMEO AND JULIET, Act II., Sc. 2.

In the quarto and folio editions, the word *runaway's* is written in the ancient fashion, "runawayes," and the point at issue has been to ascertain whom Shakespeare meant to indicate by this appellation. To exhibit the full variety of discussion, in which Shakespeare's editors and annotators have indulged upon this subject, would be to display quite a voluminous mass of laborious, if not ingenious criticism, and the course of opinion revealed affords a very curious specimen of hopeless conjecture. Whoever desires to consult the older authorities, on this point, will find them stated at length, in the Variorum edition of the poet's works; while a very ample, elaborate and able article on the subject, containing references to the more modern suggestions of critics, in England and this country, may be seen in the "Shakespeare's Scholar" of Mr. Richard Grant White, pp. 372, 387.

Mr. Singer, in his note on this passage, says that "Dr. Warburton thought that the *runaway* in question was the *sun;* but Mr. Heath has most completely disproved this opinion,"—on the ground, that Juliet could not consistently complain of the tardiness of the sun, or Phœbus, to whom she had just before assigned "fiery-footed steeds." Douce, it seems, insists that Juliet applies the term to herself, as a runaway from her duty to her parents. Monck Mason proposed *Renomy's*, that is *Renomé's;* Zachary Jackson, *unawares*, which was adopted by Collier and Knight; Dyce suggested *rude day's*, and, being dissatisfied himself with this explanation, subsequently wanders off amongst "*roving* eyes;" which he likes not much better. Steevens, with some touch of poetical instinct, clings manfully to *runaway's*, though evidently not understanding the meaning of the allusion. Mr. Halpin agrees with this, and thinks the phrase applies to Cupid, "Venus' Runaway," so styled by Moschus, and, after him, by Ben Johnson; which theory, at least, conveys an intelligible and poetical meaning, with this objection, however, that Cupid's eyes, on the occasion, ought to be open, rather than shut. It appears, however, that Mr. Heath, long ago, conjectured the word to be a misprint for "Rumour's." With this Mr. Singer now substantially coincides, substituting, however, *rumourer's;* and Mr. White, who had originally believed that this "incomprehensible runaway" was an error, which would "probably remain forever uncorrected," at last falls in with the conjecture of Mr. Heath, and asks if there "can be any doubt, that *rumoure's eyes* were the words written by the poet?"

Now, in order to explain this passage, if possible, let us resolve it into different language, conveying precisely the same ideas throughout; and it may stand thus,—

Make your best haste, oh swift steeds of the sun, to be stalled, for the night, at the mansion of Phœbus, in the West. If such a wagoner, as Phaeton once of old was, only had the reins, he would put you to your mettle, and, under the whip, would you dash through heaven to your place of rest, and bring on night at once. Now, let it be so, love-performing night! Thus, now, as then, quickly spread thy close curtain,—that runaway's eyes may wink! Such be the speed! Let this fiery charioteer—this runaway wagoner,—this Phaeton, runaway with by the steeds of the sun—perform the same feat now, (successfully)—forthwith let him wink—close his eyes—sleep—be it speedily night,—that, under its shadow, Romeo may—

Leap to these arms, untalked of and unseen!

This I conceive to have been the course of thought in Shakespeare's mind. The metonomy, in the last line, constitutes no objection to this explanation. "Unseen" would be the ordinary consequence of darkness; and so, therefore, would be "untalked of;" and, although *observation*, in the natural course of events, would precede *discussion*,—yet, for poetical purposes, surely, nothing can be more common than such a reversal of the actual "order of *their* going." The word "wink," of course, is used for sleep, in the common sense in which we employ it, e. g., *I have not slept a wink.*

And, although I do not conceive, in regard to this, or any other passage of Shakespeare, that it is essential for us to make it, as precisely and consecutively consequential, as the propositions of a syllogism,—yet, on the other hand, if it be objected that, whether Phœbus or Phaeton drive the chariot of heaven through its stages, it is the absence of the sun which causes night,—and that, therefore, in the order of nature, it is not logically consecutive, to supplicate Night to spread her curtain, in order that the eyes of *him* may wink, whose metaphorical retirement to repose is simultaneous and coincident with the action prayed for, and who is, of himself, the potential cause of this very effect of darkness,—yet, figuratively speaking, and in reference to the personification of the sun, as Phœbus or Phaeton, it was sufficiently so, and indeed it was strictly accurate for the poet so to form the imagination of it, and so to beseech Night to draw her curtain over the face of things, after heaven's charioteer had completed his course and stabled his steeds; and especially as, in this instance, after his somewhat break-neck drive, he might not unreasonably be thought in need of his natural rest.

Although, therefore, in conceiving of the ordinary succession of day and night, regarded as natural events, we are conscious that, only upon the winking of "day's garish eye," does night ensue,—and the obvious idea, in this aspect of the case, is, not that the *winking* in question follows upon, but accompanies the coming on of night,—yet, otherwise, when we think of the sun as Phœbus, or, as in this instance, as Phaeton, driving his car to the West, as his goal,—which presents the image of "civil-suited Night" coming forward to spread her close curtain behind him, only when the wagoner has arrived at his wonted mansion and has disappeared within.

The observation of Mr. Heath, therefore, on Bishop

Warburton's note, though literally correct, is not poetically so. In fact, Juliet only hints at greater speed, rather than complains of the tardiness of the sun. She addresses his coursers as *fiery-footed steeds;* but, rapid as is the movement of these flaming horses, still she would be glad to hasten their speed. The regular flight of time, to be sure, is not fast enough for her! In this consists the incompleteness and, therefore, the fallacy of Warburton's theory. However swiftly the sun,—Phœbus himself,—fulfils his ordinary course, under his government the procession of the hours is uniform and orderly; and the pace, though rapid, subject to strict guidance and control. In no proper sense, consequently, can the sun itself be denominated a "runaway;" and *ergo*, as our friend Launcelot Gobbo would say, Shakespeare did not thus offend against propriety and the nature of things. But, upon the fancy of Juliet, yearning as she was for the moment when she was to be with her lover, flashed the idea of that irregular, meteoric race through the skies, which once called for the intervention of Jove's dread thunderbolt, to stay its progress; and if the unskilful charioteer, on this occasion, were not a "runaway," and, *par excellence*, *the runaway*, in this special connection, when we are speaking of the flight of time, and seeking to accelerate its progress, we know not where Shakespeare could have looked, for so fit an example; especially when this runaway sally is the very subject of his fancy; and its chief actor is the very agent Juliet instances, and, we may presume, is wishing for, to hasten matters to the conclusion she so desired. For, in her fantastical imagination, at the hint of the name, Phœbus becomes Phaeton; this idea fills her mind, and she thus pursues the chain of thought.

The truth is, Warburton is the only one of Shakespeare's commentators, who seems to have had a glimpse of the poet's idea in this passage. But, though it is strange, that what seems so obvious, should not have occurred to a scholar like himself, apparently his mind was not of a sufficiently poetical texture fully to apprehend the association of thought in the text. Most other theories seem little better than ingenious trifling.

The whole speech, in fact, is characteristically girlish, love-sick, extravagant, erratic, *Phaetonic*. We must not here, then, require Shakespeare to produce, in detail, every minute link in the chain of his earth-embracing and heaven-embracing associations, in order to enable inconsiderate eyes to follow the flight of his imagination; and he, we will suppose, imagined us capable of catching some flashes of his meaning, when his fancy touched into being those seemingly wayward and intricate, but still ever intermingling and harmonious, shapes of light.

www.ingramcontent.com/pod-product-compliance
Lightning Source LLC
LaVergne TN
LVHW010244110826
845151LV00004B/1384

* 9 7 8 1 4 2 5 5 2 3 9 2 3 *